DRIVE IT!

The Complete Book of

LONG CIRCUIT
KARTING

Mike Smith & Rodger Calvert

Foulis

Haynes

ISBN 0 85429 416 3

© Haynes Publishing Group 1985

First published 1985

A FOULIS Motoring Book

Published by:
Haynes Publishing Group
Sparkford, Yeovil, Somerset BA22 7JJ

Haynes Publications Inc.
861 Lawrence Drive, Newbury Park, California 91320 USA

Editor: Mansur Darlington
Layout design: Mike King
Dust jacket design: Phill Jennings
Printed and bound by: J. H. Haynes & Co. Ltd.

Contents

Acknowledgements 6

Foreword 7

Introduction 9

1 The History 11

2 The Governing Bodies 19

3 The Clubs and Circuits 24

4 The Class Structure 35

5 Equipment 40

6 Spectating and Photography 55

7 The Media 67

8 A Season's Competition 73

9 The World Series 1983 87

10 The Drivers 104

Useful Addresses 124

Acknowledgements

We would like to take this opportunity to thank certain people who have helped in various ways during the preparation of this book. Firstly, we would like to thank Rod Grainger of the Haynes Publishing Group who initially obtained approval for us to go ahead with the idea.

To Mansur Darlington, who took over responsibility for the book, a special thank you for his continued patience and support during the often difficult final stages.

A very big thank you to Jim and Kurt Luby of Phoenix Karts who always allowed us access to their premises and were available at almost any time to answer queries. Without their help we would have been struggling at times.

Thanks to all the event organisers and circuit managements for supplying information and all the necessary passes.

To Zip, Ed Duckett Racing, Sisley, Stratos, and Spyda, thanks for allowing us access for photographic purposes.

To Alan Burgess thanks for his permission to use information contained in his book, *Going Karting*, and for allowing us to use extracts from *Karting Magazine*.

To Chris Lambden, Derek Rodgers and Kurt Luby thank you for your contribution to the Circuits Section.

In using the word Superkart in the text we acknowledge the fact that the word is a registered trade mark in the name of the Cadwell Car and Kart Club. Thanks to Chas Wilkinson and John Shaw for giving us permission to use it.

To the RAC and CIK, thanks for giving us permission to use their 1983 Year Books, any rules quoted are taken from that year's publication.

On the photographic side thanks to Fred Scatley, John Marshall, Les Loakes and Dennis Callingham.

A special thank you to Reg Gange for writing the Foreword, for his help in many other ways and for his great contribution in helping to make karting what it is today.

Finally, thanks to Jean for her help throughout the exercise and for keeping us both fed and watered at various times.

Mike Smith and Rodger Calvert, 1984

Foreword

I have been racing karts since the early sixties and have seen them change from 'flying bedsteads' to the sophisticated racing machines we have today. Over the last twenty years or so the sport has become much more professional — some may say, for the worse, — but I believe that if you are going to race, be it a bike, car or kart, then you must take pride in the sport and present it well. Others will, one hopes, follow your example and the general image will improve. After all if you don't take yourself seriously, who will? Inevitably, the cost of racing karts has risen, but then what hasn't? I still believe it offers an inexpensive form of competitive racing when compared with, say, Formula Ford, and it is quicker!

Personally, I have been fortunate in having some financial assistance over the years. First my Father footed the bill, then Jack Barlow of Barlotti

Reg Gange in action.

Reg Gange

Karts provided chassis for many years, whilst I had assistance from Merlin Developments on the engine side of things. After a somewhat lean spell, my very good friend, the late Martyn Merritt, sponsored my racing for two very successful seasons through his Vingt Trois Jewellery and Bullion business in Hatton Garden, London. During that period I won the World Cup at Heysham and the British Kart Grand Prix at Silverstone. The result of all that was a place in the Hermetite Zip Team run by Zip Karts of Hoddesdon. As for the future, well perhaps that depends on how often I manage to beat the Boss, Martin Hines!

I am sure this book will provide interesting reading for those who know little about kart racing and give an insight into what it is all about. Many of you could quite easily become more involved, either as spectators or participants. There is always room for additional help. For instance, a job as a voluntary marshall would certainly get you very close to the action and, believe me, you will not see any better dicing for positions in any other branch of motor sport. As well as providing excitement for spectator and driver alike, karting has a very good social side, the enthusiasts being known for their friendliness.

In closing I would like to take the opportunity to thank my faithful mechanic Graham Holloway, affectionately known as Jochen, for his valuable assistance over the past few seasons and to wish my fellow competitors the best of luck.

Let me win a few though,

see you around,

Reg Gange

EUROPEAN CHAMPION 1984

250 FORMULA E.

Introduction

Karting has been part of the motor racing scene in this country for twenty-five years and it is still both frustrating and surprising to those on the inside when they hear the mini racers referred to as go-karts. The old fairground image of a ten-pence-in-the-slot machine and a few laps round a short oval at places like Blackpool is proving very difficult to bury completely. Not that the fun karts are a bad thing, they give pleasure to a large number of people, young and old. Indeed, many who have moved into karting proper had their first taste in such a machine. It is a fact, though, that the public at large are very unsure of what karting is all about and look upon karts as kids' playthings. We very much hope, therefore, that this book will go some way toward erasing that idea once and for all.

The sport has, like all others, had its ups and downs but over the last seven or eight years, with the increased use of full-size motor racing circuits, karting has shown itself to be an excellent branch of racing and at last the message is getting across. National and world prestige events such as the CIK World Series, the European Championship and the British Kart Grand Prix have all contributed to getting karting its proper and deserved recognition. Racing is racing at whatever level and the smell of Castrol R is just as strong at a kart meeting as it is for an F3 event. The small size of the karts should not deceive you either, for with speeds of up to 140 mph the top class of 250cc Superkarts can more than match their more glamorous brethren in terms of acceleration, road holding and, more importantly, spectacle. The class structure has evolved over the last twenty-five years to its present state of having just four categories racing on long circuits.

The oldest class, one often referred to as the backbone of British karting, is the 210 National category which utilises in most cases modern replicas of the original 197cc Villiers enlarged to 210cc. That engine was used in the old blue invalid carriage and is being asked to perform way above what was first intended. It does provide, however, some good and inexpensive racing for a large number of people and is an essential part of long circuit racing. The next class in terms of engine size is the 125cc category which, since being allowed on to full-size motor racing circuits towards the end of the seventies, has gone from strength to strength with entries approaching the 100 mark at some events. Using the Austrian Rotax engine, the class provides some highly entertaining and spectacular racing with up to sixty karts on the starting grid. The competition is close, incidents are numerous and speeds are high.

The next higher class is the 250 National Class which is for karts powered by single-cylinder engines with a maximum capacity of 250cc. Once the premier class of British karting the advent of the use of Japanese twin-cylinder machines in international competition led to serious decline of the single cylinder class's popularity. The last two or three years, though, has seen a revival of interest and, using the Yamaha YZ 250 G air-cooled engine, drivers in this class are once again providing some close wheel-to-wheel racing.

Finally, we come to the premier class in long circuit karting, that of 250 Formula E, which has become widely known as the Superkart Class. The Cadwell Park management introduced the term Superkart in the late seventies in an effort to improve the public image of the top class. At that time Superbikes had become an accepted part of the bike racing scene and it was thought that karting should follow that lead. Thus, the word Superkart was duly registered as a trade mark by the Cadwell Club. For sheer spectacle, power and excitement look no further than this class. With the knowledge that the Austrian Rotax engine produces some 70 bhp it doesn't need too much imagination to visualize the excitement caused by the sound and sight of thirty or forty Superkarts screaming off the line at the start of yet another final. Increased television coverage has helped tremendously to improve the image of long circuit karting with the Superkarts taking part in a series of special events for television from Donington Park.

Karting on long circuits has gradually grown to the point where it has become totally separated from the rest of karting. It is a fact that the number of licence holders who are regularly active around the motor racing circuits account for only around 10% of the total. The 10%, though, form a closely knit, extremely competitive, yet extremely friendly bunch of addicts. Driver and spectator share a close affinity, the result being that kart meetings are generally very open affairs. The public can wander freely around the pit and paddock area and soak up the atmosphere of race day. It is a world of very specialized machinery, karts can be used for racing only, but it is also a world where almost everyone will readily exchange ideas and offer assistance.

1 The History

In tracing the history of karting one has to go back about twenty-eight years to the Kurtis Craft Company in Glendale, California. It was there that an employee of the company, Art Ingels, spent his days assisting in the building of racing cars for events such as the world famous Indianapolis. Working with the same steel tubing used in the construction of those racing cars, Ingels built the first ever kart around August of 1956.

His first creation was of a very simple design; two straight side rails joined by a straight front axle across one end and a tube containing axle stubs at the rear. A simple steering hoop, a three spoke steering wheel and a column with a steering spade and two drag links finished it all off. The engine was a West Bend Model 750 which had been bought from Flexo Products of Los Angeles. Flexo had acquired about 8000 similar units, originating from McCulloch-produced rotary mowers. The mowers, unfortunately, were not a success and after complaints started to pour in McCulloch decided to scrap the whole thing. The engines were destined to spend some time in storage until Flexo stepped in.

Once completed and running, Ingels' creation was tested in car parks and school playgrounds before the big day arrived and it was taken to a car race meeting at Pamona in September of that year. Spectating at that event was a gentleman by the name of Duffy Livingstone who was in business with Roy Desbrow manufacturing and repairing car exhaust systems. Livingstone was impressed by Ingels mini racer and almost immediately after returning home from the event put his mind to working out details of constructing one himself. Two karts were initially put together by Livingstone, one for himself and

one for Dick Van de Veere, the latter being given the task of locating all the necessary parts. Ingels' meanwhile, was attracting a lot of attention with his project and everyone who saw it was impressed with the performance from such a small motor. The West Bend was just 2½ hp; and bearing in mind that Ingels weighed in at around fifteen stone there was some justification for being impressed. Ingels had installed the motor directly behind the driver and forward motion was achieved by a centrifugal clutch and a small countershaft. The fuel tank was mounted high, again behind the driver and there was only one foot operated pedal ... the accelerator. Braking was by means of a lever on the right hand side which operated a plate so positioned that it pressed on the rear tyre.

Over the next few months all manner of problems occurred; the tiny engines repeatedly blew up; frames proved not strong enough and sagged; brakes were prone to complete failure, and numerous bits and pieces just simply fell off! Enthusiasm, however, remained very high and by March 1957 there was an eager band of about ten or a dozen kart owners itching to get out there and race the things. Once again, school playgrounds and car parks were the favoured venues, and each Sunday the owners would meet and set off in search of somewhere to run. All went well until the local police arrived to move them on and threaten dire consequences if they dared to return. After a couple of months of constantly being shoved around, a breakthrough came with the discovery of the Rose Bowl car park in Pasadena. At last the drivers were able to drive around free of police interference. Passing motorists soon began to stop and view with interest the goings on and gradually enquiries

11

started coming in from people wanting to buy their own kart. Livingstone and Desbrow finally agreed to make up a kit of parts for sale to the public with the customer having to do welding etc. in order to assemble the kart. At that time a West Bend engine, all the tubing bent to shape, wheels and all the other necessary bits could be bought for the princely sum of £43.

The next significant milestone in the progress of this new sport was the involvement of *Rod and Custom* magazine through its Art Director, Lynn Wineland, and Editor Spencer Murray. The two of them did much to further promote the sport by running articles and editorial features in the magazine. Desbrow and Livingstone required a name for their new product and, after talking with Wineland and Spencer, the name Go Kart was agreed with the Go Kart Company being formed to market the product. The *Rod and Custom* men helped further by producing a sort of sales brochure and very soon Go Kart were selling 500 kits per month. Ingels, meanwhile, had not been idling his time away and had been trying very hard to interest his boss at Kurtis Craft in the manufacture of karts. The idea failed to impress and eventually Ingels decided to leave the Company and join forces with Lou Borelli. A company was formed and production started with their creation being called the Caretta.

By December of 1957 the Go Kart Club of America was formed and the sport began to take on a much more organised appearance. Rules were formulated governing the size of chassis and engines and the word was spreading fast ... even beyond America.

It was not long before that news reached England, initially through the United States Air Force bases where a Staff Sergeant, Micky Flynn, read of the happenings back home whilst stationed at Burton Wood. Supported by his wife, Pat, Flynn gave consideration to the idea of

Cadwell Park in Lincolnshire has been involved with karting for over twenty years.

Narrow tyres, a wide wheelbase and a lay down driving position. Mid sixties style.

An example of the ingenuity shown by drivers competing in the Snetterton 9 Hours. This kart is unusual in having the engine at the front. Was it put there to keep the driver warm?

A further change from the conventional. A right-hand mounted engine.

bringing karts over to England, and in July of 1958 they took the plunge and sent off an order to Livingstone at the Go Kart Company for five kits. By September the kits had arrived and assembly operations started almost at once. Fitted with Clinton engines they made their début around American Air Force bases and quickly aroused a lot of interest amongst service personnel. In no time, news spread and, helped by further articles in motor magazines sent over from America, a sudden rush of kart building began from interested home-based parties.

As far as it is known the first kart to be built in this country (apart from those kits brought in by Flynn) was that produced by Ecurie Minima of Bristol. Quite independently of each other, karts were also soon being produced by Skeeta at Sandford, Motor Karts of Surbiton and Speedex of Luton. Almost a year after he had first introduced the kart to USAF bases Flynn obtained permission to run the first organised race meeting after giving a demonstration to the 'top brass'.

In August of 1959 the breakthrough came for karting in this country. A demonstration of karts was given in front of the pits at a car meeting at Silverstone. Sufficient interest was created as a result that a meeting was called by the RAC to try and draw up a set of competition rules. That meeting, in September 1959, was attended by a representative of the Villiers Company and at the outset British rules included provision for a class with gearbox. Interest from the RAC, motorsports governing body, and from a major engine manufacturer meant that the sport was on its way. Two wildly enthusiastic people, Albert Zains and John Hume, had combined forces as a result of that Silverstone meeting and started producing the Azum kart. It was their next move though, that was to have more wide-reaching results. They placed an advert in *Autosport* magazine announcing that they had hired Brands Hatch and were to put on a display to show everyone what karting was all about. A rather crude track was laid out on the main straight and all and sundry had the opportunity to try the products from various manufacturers. The whole scene was one of chaos but the message at the end of the day was clear; karting had caught the public's imagination and looked likely to stay. A couple of months later and it was once more the turn of Micky Flynn to contribute to the movement when he ran the first ever race meeting in this country. That took place at Lakenheath in November 1959 and was attended by all of the so-called 'works' teams of that time. Included amongst the drivers was none other than Graham Hill, driving for the Progress Team.

By the beginning of 1960 production of karts for sale to the public had begun in earnest and many would-be manufacturers appeared to take advantage of the growing sport. As is often the case with a new interest many were to fall by the wayside, but the more genuine ones survived until production was in full swing.

Because it is the gearbox scene with which we are concerned in this book we will concentrate on the progress of Class 4, as it was known initially. Class 1 was for karts with direct drive

An example of the Bultaco engine widely used in the sixties.

The transitional period single-cylinder versus twin. Brands Hatch.

The Superkarts were not the only class to have bodies, as this shot of Dud Moseley's Motus 210 shows.

Seventies style — showing alternative types of bodywork. Increased sponsorship within karting helped the image.

Increased use of bodywork allowed for more advertising space and a number of well known companies came into the sport in the mid seventies.

engines. The gearbox class was the stamping ground of the Villiers 9E engine, a unit used to power a variety of motor-cycles and the old blue invalid carriages made by Invacar Ltd, and until the Autumn of 1960 was about the only engine to be used. The Spanish Bultaco then made its entry and, producing around 20 bhp, looked set to change the face of karting overnight. In the first eighteen months of karting in the UK only short tracks were in use, many of them on old airfields, marked out with straw bales and old tyres. Motor racing circuits were being used only rarely, one of the problems being that of safety. Kart drivers were almost totally exposed and the necessary safety requirements of karting were difficult to achieve satisfactorily.

One of the first forays onto a full motor racing circuit was in May of 1960 at the Olivers Mount circuit near Scarborough. One or two similar opportunities presented themselves over the next few years but it was 1964 before regular use of the motor racing circuits occurred. Whilst the struggle for fuller recognition was a continuing battle, improvements in kart design were taking place all the time. One of the most successful designs of the period was the Fastakart which used a flat, ladder-type frame rather like many of the Class 1 outfits. Lessons were learned somewhat slowly though and it was 1966 before that type of frame caught on in a big way. The previous year, 1965, had been the time for just one simple rule change which was to have a marked effect on the structure of British karting. Class 4 became a split category with Standard and Super classifications giving the Villiers engine an outlet of its own and doing likewise for engines such as the Bultaco and Montesa.

Motor racing circuits were now playing a much more active role and meetings were being held at most of the established tracks. 1966 brought the introduction of endurance racing on a long circuit with Snetterton in Norfolk hosting the *Karting Magazine*-supported 9 Hours event. Those events gave rise to some weird and wonderful examples of karters' ingenuity and were very well supported. Throughout the history of karting, major changes affecting the sport have usually been related to engine eligibility and it was in 1968 that an important change of that type was suggested. Initially on an experimental basis it was agreed that a 250cc engine should be allowed into the sport, but at the start only those clubs with RAC permission would be allowed to run events for that size of engine. One of the top Bultaco tuners of the mid-sixties, Frank Sheene, felt that if a 250 class was allowed then karting would progress by leaps and bounds. The RAC subsequently decided that to be eligible engines must be air-cooled of between 201 and 250cc,

have no more than two cylinders and a maximum of five gears. Once the 250 class had been introduced the Spanish-built Bultaco and Montesa continued to dominate the result sheets, and it was five years before any great changes were seen to be imminent.

In 1973 Phil Hilton led the final of the British Championships on a Suzuki and the writing was on the wall for the Spanish factories. Furthermore, in the South of England those followers of karting were keenly watching the progress of the flying Doble brothers, Chris and Mike, and it was Chris who eventually took the honours with victories in all three rounds of the Championship. The power unit used was, like Hilton's, a Suzuki but the Doble example was tuned and prepared by Roy Baldwin. The engine had been on the list of eligible motors for some time as had a number of other twin-cylinder examples. All it needed was someone with the necessary expertise to turn it into a winner and Baldwin did just that.

Whilst developments in chassis design (they were no longer falling apart so readily) had played a part in the progress of karting, a pattern was emerging of each class being a one-engine class. Or, at least, that is how it appeared as one particular motor proved to be better than the others, thereby encouraging most of the top drivers to opt for that marque. Then increased use of Japanese twin-cylinder engines did mean, of course, that the previously unbeatable Spanish motors had now met their match and the RAC were forced into a situation whereby they had to come up with a separate class to accommodate those wishing to stay with the Spanish product.

By the mid-seventies then, karting had moved from its initial one-class, one-engine state to three classes each with their own approved power source. A couple of years later yet another engine size was to appear around the long circuits and this time it was one of 125cc. Previously having run only on the short specialist kart tracks, the 125 Yamaha was unleashed onto motor racing circuits. The pace setter in those early days was a Teign Valley Motors-prepared TZ125D Yamaha in the hands of Steve Elmore and mounted in a Zip chassis. So by the late seventies the class structure of British Long Circuit karting was established with a category for almost all tastes and all pockets.

Whilst the choice of engines has played such a big part in shaping the history of karting, it is also true to say that the introduction of prestige events has had a definite influence on its progress. There is always something special about a really big event and although it took place on a short circuit, at Heysham Nr. Morecambe, the World Cup from its inception in 1968 always attracted a huge entry from home and abroad and was regarded by many as THE event to win. Bert Hesketh, a stalwart of Northern gearbox karting, was responsible for that event and it was Bert who also introduced the European Championship in 1976, this time running the first event at Oulton Park. A couple of years after that, Silverstone was to play a major role in helping karting to really make its mark by agreeing to run, with help from the Daily Express and Hermetite Products, a British Kart Grand Prix. The RAC gave it full Grand Prix status and it became Britain's third properly sanctioned Grand Prix. Cadwell Park was perhaps the one other circuit to play an important part in the development of karting on long circuits as its management at last agreed to allow the karts to run on the full 2¼ mile circuit. The late Sydney Taylor was Secretary of the Cadwell Club at the time and he felt that the karts would be a workable proposition on motor racing circuits. A new image was needed, though, and after much thought the word Superkart was introduced and registered as a trade mark in the name of the Cadwell Club. It was felt that following the success of the Superbike image a similar title for the 250 karts would help to promote the cause with the general public. Regulations were formed for Cadwell meetings stating that to be eligible for the Superkart Class, karts must have some form of bodywork. Martin Hines of Zip Karts, always an innovator, was quick to grasp the situation and was soon producing various items of fibreglass for bolting on to the karts. Front nose cones, rear wings, side tanks and pods soon became the accepted thing and karts took on a new and attractive appearance. With the increased use of fibreglass there was more flat areas for advertising purposes and here again Hines was one of the first to tie up a substantial sponsorship deal. Coupled with their previous motor racing interests, Hermetite Products of West Drayton took an interest in karting, and the start of 1976 saw Hines and his Zip in that Company's colours. Sponsorship had arrived. The Hermetite involvement was not the only development of note at the beginning of the '76 season for at the first meeting, Cadwell Park in February, Hines turned out on a twin-cylinder Yamaha and the face of karting was to change yet again. Over the next five years the Yamaha was to prove just about unbeatable, although one or two Suzukis still managed to make their mark, as at the World Cup in 1976 when Dave Buttigieg won on a Barlotti chassis with Suzuki power.

As the seventies moved towards the eighties the sport appeared to be in a reasonably stable condition. The Villiers was still going strong albeit mainly with modern replicas of the original; the 125 class was growing and becoming increasingly popular whilst the 250 National Class

Hermetite sponsorship, Yamaha power and Hines in the driving seat proved to be a winning combination.

Formula One driver, Nigel Mansell, began his motor racing in the Villiers Class. Seen here chatting to John Newton at a Cadwell meeting.

A more recent recruit to Formula 1, Brazilian Ayrton Senna, also began his career in karts, albeit in Class One.

was the category most in need of some help and, perhaps, a new engine. The late seventies also brought about a dramatic change in the construction and availability of tyres. Long established names such as Goodyear and Dunlop were suddenly to find themselves with some stiff opposition as the Japanese Bridgestone Tyre Company introduced its wares to British karting.

The next significant change concerned an engine change and came about in 1981. The previous year much discussion, indeed argument, took place of whether or not to adopt the proposal of a change in the 250 class to water-cooled engines. Eventually the proposal was adopted, marking another important waypoint in karting's history. The engine in question was the Austrian-produced Rotax Model 256 and, once the early teething problems had been overcome, it quickly proved to be exciting and competitive. The previously successful air-cooled Yamaha was made uncompetitive overnight and, although one or two drivers switched to the water-cooled variety of Japanese motor, the Rotax remained dominant. Its smaller stable mate, the 125cc model 124 Rotax has also made huge inroads in the smaller capacity class and has proved to be the engine to have if you wish to be successful at that level.

Although it may be nice to have stability in any sport one cannot halt progress and already there is a possibility of yet more changes, again in the engine department for 1985. This time though it concerns the single-cylinder 250 category with the possibility that water-cooled engines may be adopted for this class too. The most recent

Before the change to water-cooling, Derek Price caused a stir when he campaigned a Sprint powered by TWO 125cc engines.

As Rotax power came in so did some rather eye catching designs in bodywork. This example on the Aero of Steve Styrin was one of the most attractive at the time.

change in the 125 class concerns a new motor approved for use after November 1st 1984. This is the Italian Minarelli which is being imported by Jim and Kurt Luby through their Phoenix Kart business. Only the 1985 season will tell how successful this new engine proves to be. On the events front, well, 1983 brought us the first ever CIK officially recognised World Championship and it was our own Martin Hines who brought that title back home as the World's No.1.

The shape of Martin Hines' 1983 World Championship winning outfit.

2 The Governing Bodies

Any form of sport must have a governing body responsible for formulating the rules and regulations and to see that those rules are applied. In that respect karting in this country is looked after by the RAC Motor Sports Association Ltd from its offices in Belgrave Square, London. The RAC MSA has a full time staff employed at those offices and is engaged in all aspects of motor sport from Autocross to Grand Prix racing.

In addition to being the ASN (National Sporting Authority) for British motor sport, the RAC MSA is also the organising club for this country's four major events; the British Formula 1 Grand Prix; the RAC Rally; the London to Brighton Run and (the one we are most interested in), the British Kart Grand Prix. The RAC MSA has undergone some important changes over the years, not least of which was the formation of a limited company with effect from January 1979. Four years earlier a Motor Sports Council had been formed and given much wider powers than the former Competitions Committee. The Council is made up of a chairman and three other people nominated by the Royal Automobile Club together with the chairman of each of the specialist committees. In addition, representatives from the motor industry and circuit owners take their place on the Council. With the rather more specialist knowledge required to administer adequately all the various forms of four-wheeled sport in this country, separate committees have been set up to look after the interests of each section.

Each committee is the responsibility of one member of the Executive staff and for karting that person is Mr Robert Langford. The kart committee has a total of twelve members under the chairmanship of Mr Michael Southecombe and meets about every two months. Members are not elected to the committee but take their place by invitation and a good cross-section of all aspects of karting is represented on the committee. All members have a wide and varied knowledge of karting ranging from the manufacture of karts to the organisation of race meetings. It is through its kart committee, therefore, that the RAC MSA must attempt to ensure that the sport is running smoothly and the licence holders are happy. With around three and a half thousand kart licences issued in 1983 that is no easy task, for each of those licence holders may have his own views as to how his activities should be controlled.

In order to compete in events one must first have a properly organised meeting to attend and here again the RAC MSA is responsible for authorising events through recognised clubs. Taking into account all branches, including short and long circuit events, there are about fifty officially recognised karting clubs, some, of course, more active than others. Before embarking on a kart racing foray a competition licence must be obtained from the RAC. Kart competition licences are available either for kart circuits or for both kart circuits and long circuits. The latter are recognised motor racing circuits or tracks exceeding 1500 metres in length. Short circuit licences are issued from the age of 10 and are in two grades: Novice and International. Until a driver has competed in 4 events to the satisfaction of the Steward, obtained the necessary signatures and had his licence upgraded to International Short Circuit he will be regarded as a Novice.

Once in possession of that International Licence a driver can then compete on long circuits as a Novice provided he has reached the age of 17. Additionally, he must be in possession of a

The main entrance to the RAC Motor Sports association offices in Belgrave Square, London.

Mr Robert Langford who is Karting Executive at the RAC and a member of the CIK.

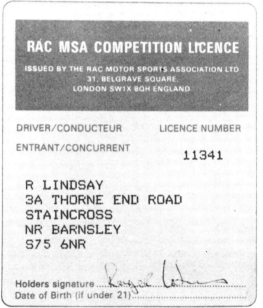

20   The aim of all novice kart drivers, an International Kart Licence issued by the RAC.

Road Traffic Act Licence (an ordinary road driving licence) and have competed satisfactorily in at least two gearbox events on short kart circuits. A full kart licence is also split into two grades; Novice and International, and is valid for both short and long circuits. A full licence is only issued to competitors who have reached the age of 17 and hold a full road licence. A Novice kart licence holder must have competed to the satisfaction of the Stewards in at least 4 short circuit gearbox events before being allowed to compete in a motor racing circuit event. Finally, to compete on long circuit events a medical certificate must be acquired.

On receipt of your first licence you will be sent a copy of the RAC MSA Yearbook. This publication is really the competitors' 'bible' and is commonly referred to as the Blue Book. No, it is not pornographic! It covers all branches of motor sport under the jurisdiction of the RAC and includes all the relevant technical regulations relating to the sport. Changes in rules are usually avoided during a racing season except where the prime consideration is one of safety. Here again the RAC MSA issues a news sheet to all competitors containing such items as they occur.

The karting press also plays its part by publicising any important news to come from Belgrave Square. Although the foregoing information on the licencing structure may appear rather complicated, in practice it is not as daunting as it seems and in all cases advice will be readily available should you have any particular problem.

As well as being the licensing body for drivers, circuits and officials, the RAC MSA also has to deal with any disputes arising from the actions of competitors or from scrutineering, that is, questions of eligibility relating to equipment. There is a set procedure for the lodging of protests and the hearing of subsequent appeals and if a dispute cannot be settled on the day at the circuit then it is referred to Belgrave Square for an official ruling. Fortunately, that sort of problem does not arise too often at kart meetings but it is nice to know that a system does exist for settling such happenings when they occur. On home circuits the RAC is responsible for the annual championships in each class of karting and these are allocated to various clubs at the start of the season. In the past, long circuit racing has had one day championships but in recent years that has been replaced by a multi-round series taking place on various circuits with all the regular organising clubs involved in staging one or more rounds. A points system is used with currently five out of six rounds to count and the man with the most points at the end becomes the RAC British Champion for his class. To win the British

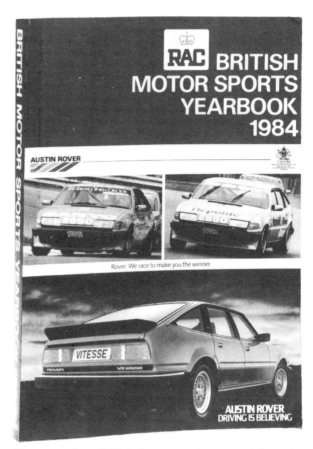

The competitors 'bible'. Issued to all licence holders but perhaps not as widely read as it should be!

Championship entitles the holder to use one of the coveted special number plates, and as befits the title the No. 1 plate is carried by that driver for the following season.

There is one other very important area where the RAC MSA is involved and that is the prestigious British Kart Grand Prix at Silverstone. Since its introduction to the long circuit racing calendar in 1978 the Grand Prix has been organised by the RAC MSA and the full administrative capacity of the governing body has ensured its continued success. With the help of Silverstone circuit and members of the Blackpool and Fylde Club the weekend has become acknowledged as the highlight of the karting year. We shall however be looking at that more closely later.

On the international karting scene a second governing body comes into the arena in the form of the Commission Internationale de Karting. More usually referred to in the abbreviated form as simply the CIK it is responsible, as its title suggests, for the control and administration of karting at international level. In doing that it appoints the various ASN's mentioned earlier to carry through the international regulations in each country. In Britain that role is taken on by the

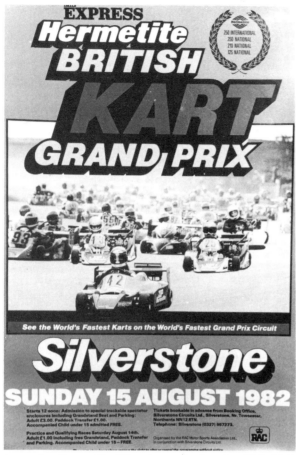

In conjunction with Silverstone circuits the RAC MSA organises the British Kart Grand Prix.

The CIK Yearbook, a must for any competitors intending to race to International Regulations at world level.

Switzerland's Ernest Buser, President of the CIK, and one of the major figures in the promotion of Formula E at world level.

RAC. As far as this country is concerned, the 250 Formula E class, or Superkarts, is controlled by CIK regulations which do differ in some respects to the national class regulations. Some 35 countries are represented on the CIK with Britain's representatives being the RAC kart executive, Robert Langford, and Derek Ongaro as the deputy representative. Robert Langford is also a member of the CIK committee. The president of the CIK is Switzerland's Ernest Buser and he has shown a very keen interest in furthering world competition in the Superkart class. Indeed, he was very much involved in helping to establish the first CIK officially recognised 250 Formula E World Championship which is dealt with in more detail later.

As in the case of the RAC, the CIK publish annually a yearbook for karting: the Annuaire du Karting. Whilst the RAC Blue Book contains all the relevant information regarding national racing the CIK publication gives all those rules applicable to international competition. It is printed in French but does carry an English translation so you do not need to be bi-lingual to understand the text. It is, however, worth remembering that only the French text is considered to be the authentic one. Copies can usually be obtained from the offices of the RAC in London but for those who may wish to apply direct the address to write to is; Commission Internationale de Karting, 8. Place de la Concorde, Paris.

As in the case of the RAC being responsible for the British Championships, so the CIK is the body engaged in administering both the European and World Championships. For the gearbox and long circuit karters only the 250 Formula E class, Superkarts, are catered for at that level. Until 1983 only the European Championship was held but, with the enthusiasm of the president, M. Buser, together with trade representatives, a plan was produced for the first ever CIK recognised World Championship for Formula E. That took place in 1983 and was run under CIK rules. We will look at that series of events in more detail in a later chapter.

Finally, even if you are not in any way involved in karting, you can attend the annual RAC Kart Open Day. That was, until 1983, held in London on a weekday but that year was moved to a Saturday and held at Donington Park racing circuit. Attendance offers those present a chance to put their questions and views on any aspect of the sport to representatives of the governing body. Items for general discussion are on the agenda also and it is your chance to have your say. Sadly, the open day is not generally well supported, which is a pity really for it is the one occasion, other than on race days, when a good cross-section of all spheres of karting can be assembled under one roof.

A change of venue in 1983 took the Annual RAC Kart Open Day to the Midlands racing circuit at Donington Park.

3 The Clubs and Circuits

Having looked at the bodies responsible for the administration of karting at both national and international level we will now turn our attentions to the organising clubs and the circuits on which they operate. We will chiefly be concerned with those clubs which look after the racing on the full motor racing venues, but it should be remembered that on the short circuit scene there is a multitude of local clubs and tracks catering for the needs of karters in virtually every corner of the country. In fact, the RAC Motor Sports Year Book lists some fifty clubs currently involved in the running of meetings and further lists all those tracks approved for racing.

It has been said that in many cases the most accomplished of drivers on the long circuits learned their skills on the tighter confines of the shorter kart tracks. With the coming of more powerful machinery, especially in the 250 Formula E class, the drift away from short tracks has been more noticeable in recent years although many of the gearbox drivers do still take part at the purpose built kart tracks. In looking at the organisational side of kart racing you will see that the whole of the racing on full motor racing circuits is in the hands of just three or four clubs.

At its home base in Lincolnshire the Cadwell Car and Kart Club, as expected, looks after the interests of karters at Cadwell Park. The Central Kart Club is responsible for the running of meetings at Snetterton in Norfolk, Brands Hatch in Kent and Mallory Park in Leicestershire. The Blackpool and Fylde Club is at the helm for meetings at Oulton Park in addition to looking after the TV events at Donington Park and assisting with the administration on race day at the Silverstone Grand Prix weekend. The RAC Motor Sports Association is the organising club

for that once a year Grand Prix spectacular. We will look first, though, at the circuit which regularly hosts the greatest number of kart events, five in all, that is, Cadwell Park.

Cadwell Park

Situated just off the A 153 road between Louth and Horncastle in Lincolnshire the circuit is set in beautiful undulating parkland with ample space for camping and caravanning. The full circuit is 2¼ miles in length and offers a wide variety of straights, sweeping bends and tight, first gear hairpins. It has often been likened to a mini Nürburgring with its many ups and downs, and it is recognised that to win at Cadwell calls for a high degree of skill.

Karts have raced at the Lincolnshire venue for 22 years. The late Sydney Taylor, who was secretary of the Car and Kart Club, had much to do with the progress nationally of karting on motor racing circuits. It was he who came up with the word Superkart to describe the new breed of colourful twin cylinder outfits in the mid seventies. On the death of Sydney Taylor karting was robbed of one of its strongest supporters; many people regard Cadwell as Syd Taylor's circuit.

It was John Shaw who took over the task of running Cadwell meetings as the new secretary of the club and, as is the case of all such clubs, John has built up a good team of mainly voluntary helpers to ensure the continuance of racing at this popular venue. Within its 2¼ miles Cadwell can, by use of short links, bring into use two further circuits; the 1½ mile Club circuit and the 1 mile Woodlands circuit. Both use the link opposite the Grandstand towards the end of the main straight,

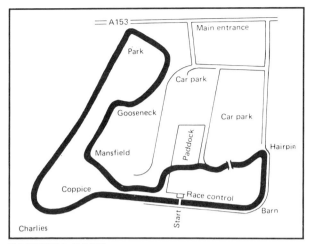

CADWELL PARK

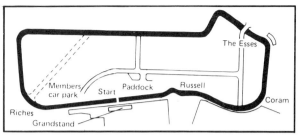

SNETTERTON

the club circuit turning right to go back up Coppice Hill whilst the Woodlands circuit uses the main straight turning right once more but into the Mountain section and then through the wooded part of the course. Cadwell has traditionally opened the kart racing season with a meeting on the last Sunday in February and often it is a case of all hands to the shovels as snow is cleared from the track and surrounding areas. Further meetings are usually held on Easter Sunday each year, June, August and October.

In view of the demanding nature of the track, speeds attained on any one of the three circuits are quite high with the lap record for Superkarts on the full circuit standing at 1m 27.1s with a speed of 92.99 mph and set by Dave Buttigieg in August 1982. The same driver also holds the record for the shorter Club circuit at a speed of exactly 90 mph, a time of just 1 minute. Cadwell is one of the few circuits in the country to remain in private ownership. It is still in the hands of the Wilkinson family of which Mr Charles Wilkinson is chairman of the Kart Club and often in attendance at meetings. Although the off track facilities leave something to be desired there is no doubt that Cadwell is a popular venue and over the years has done much to further the cause of gearbox karting on motor racing circuits.

There are many excellent vantage points from which one can watch the racing at close quarters, the Club circuit hairpin and the Mountain section on the full circuit being two of the most popular spots. To see a kart airborne at the top of the Mountain is a sight not to be missed.

Snetterton
Moving on into Norfolk we will now look at the first of the three circuits at which the Central Kart Club operates. Formerly a wartime airfield, Snetterton is situated off the A 11 Thetford to

Norwich road and, like Cadwell, has ample space for those wishing to camp. The circuit is 1.917 miles in length and being an old airfield is mainly fairly flat except for the drop down to Russell Bend from Coram Curve. Due to its somewhat isolated position it is not the best of circuits to get to but, nevertheless, the Central Kart Club regularly hold two or three meetings each year, all being fairly well supported. Snetterton is owned by Motor Circuit Development who also own Brands Hatch and Oulton Park. Its remote location does have one advantage though and that is that it is not troubled by complaints over noise. Indeed, Snetterton did for a number of years host the very popular 9 hour events.

Within the paddock area there is a clubhouse and cafe, both of which are open on practice and race days providing competitors and spectators with much needed refreshment. Lap speeds are much higher than on the tighter Cadwell circuit and the Superkarts lap at around 105 mph! The organisation of meetings is in the hands of the locally-based Central Kart Club of which the Secretary, Ian Rushforth, and Clerk of the Course, Peter Carter, are, like many officials, former kart drivers. Meetings are usually held in March, April and September though, like most of the circuits used, dates have to be flexible to fit in with the overall pattern of the season's motor racing generally.

Brands Hatch
The second of the three venues visited by the Central Club is this world famous Grand Prix circuit in Kent and another of the MCD circuits. Situated off the A 20 between Swanley and Wrotham, Brands Hatch is a hive of activity throughout the year. Unfortunately, karts are able to use the circuit only once a year except for the occasions when Superkarts take part in a British Racing and Sports Car Club event.

The 1.2 mile Indy circuit is used and offers perhaps the best viewing of any circuit in Britain. From a position opposite the pit lane garages or overlooking Paddock Hill Bend virtually all of the Indy circuit can be seen and progress of your favourite driver carefully noted. The facilities are,

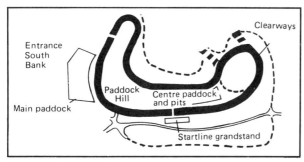

BRANDS HATCH

of course, first class with numerous sales points and the Kentagon building in which one can take ample refreshment. Brands Hatch was involved in karting many years ago, in fact, one of the first ever demonstrations of the sport took place at the Kent circuit. The circuit was for a considerable time not available to karters and it is only during the last couple of years that events have again been held there.

Mallory Park

If we now move back up to the Midlands we come to the last of the Central Kart Club's venues. In 1982 it looked very much as though this Leicestershire circuit was to be lost forever to motor racing fans. Motor Circuit Developments decided that they could no longer carry the losses incurred and put the site up for sale. However, into the arena stepped a leading sports car driver, Chris Meek, and through his company, Titan Properties, Mallory Park had a new owner. The parent company is Post Castle Properties and the organisation of the circuit is in the hands of the Midlands Branch of the British Racing and Sports Car Club.

MALLORY PARK

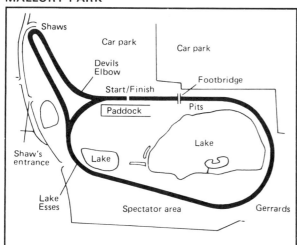

The circuit is situated just nine miles from Junction 21 on the M1 near Hinkley and Earl Shilton and is 1.35 miles in length. Its central position makes it a very popular venue with both competitors and spectators. Rising ground opposite the main start/finish straight affords excellent viewing with only the hairpin not being visible. Facilities are good with a bar and cafeteria within the paddock area and other sales sites available on race days. The new owners have a number of further plans to improve the surroundings.

As far as the karts are concerned it is quite a fast circuit with lap speeds of around the 106 mph mark for the 250 Formula E class. For 1984 four visits were made by the karting fraternity so it would seem that Mallory is well and truly back in the motor racing game.

Donington Park

Not too far away from the Leicestershire circuit, just a short drive north on the M1 and we reach the venue that is looked after from a karting point of view by the Blackpool and Fylde Club. Donington can be reached off the A453 Nottingham to Birmingham road and is just three miles from Junction 24 on the M1. The East Midlands Airport is but a stone's throw away making the circuit very accessible whatever your choice of transport happens to be. Under the ownership of the Wheatcroft family the circuit is continually being improved with new amenities added for the comfort of both spectators and competitors. It already has an excellent motor racing museum, its own pub, at Redgate corner and a cafe. Numerous other sales points are usually open on race days.

Plans are well in hand to extend the circuit length, at present 1.957 miles, to include a new section behind the paddock area. That will bring it up to the standards required to host full Formula One Grand Prix events.

In the last couple of years this very popular

DONINGTON PARK

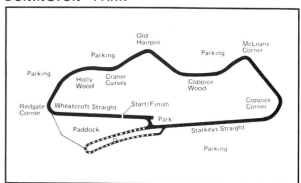

circuit has been used by the Superkarts only for the televised series and when taking part in BRSCC events. For 1984, however, to replace the World Cup classic from Heysham short circuit a new international event organised by the Blackpool and Fylde Club took place over the May Spring Bank Holiday Weekend.

The man at the helm of the Blackpool Club is one of the stalwarts of gearbox karting, Bert Hesketh. Bert has been involved in karting for many many years both at national and inter-national level and it was he who introduced the World Cup, and later the European Championship at Oulton Park.

Oulton Park

This circuit is also in the hands of Motor Circuit Developments and is near Tarporly in Cheshire, off the A 54. The track in general use in recent years was 1.654 miles in length but that was increased to 2.356 miles for the 1984 season. The new section will incorporate the fast climb to the hairpin at Island Bend and then swoop downhill to Knicker Brook. That section has been used by bike racers recently but has remained out of bounds to cars and karts.

As with all MCD circuits a local manager is in attendance and available to answer any queries.

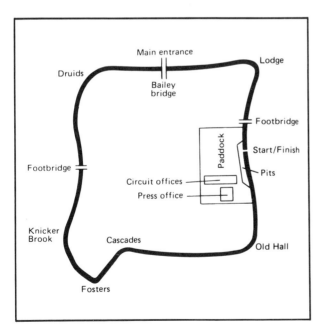

OULTON PARK

Silverstone

Known the world over by motor racing fans, is Silverstone, often described as the Home of British Motor Racing. It is situated off the A 43 between Towcester and Brackley. The full Grand

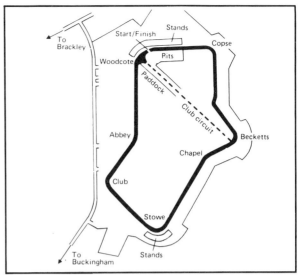

SILVERSTONE

Prix circuit is 2.927 miles in length and regarded as one of the fastest circuits in the world.

Silverstone was the scene of one of the earliest kart demonstrations in this country and in the early years of the sport meetings were held by the Rochester Motor Club. With such a full programme of events, though, the circuit was lost to karts and it was not until 1978 that karting returned to Silverstone.

Martin Hines and Silverstone's Managing Director, Jimmy Brown, had much to do with the return of karting and the establishing of the prestige event, the Kart Grand Prix. A demonstra-tion of karts had taken place at a motor-cycle Grand Prix and those watching, including representatives of Martin Hines' sponsors, Hermetite products, were impressed. The result was the British Kart Grand Prix which, over the last five years, has become the highlight of the karting calendar. The organisation of the Grand Prix is very much a shared exercise with the RAC, Silverstone Circuits and the Blackpool and Fylde Club all being involved. For such a big event, of course, additional help is brought in from numerous sources and the planning of one event starts as the previous one finishes.

As one would expect from a circuit with Silverstone's experience and status the facilities for the Grand Prix weekend are first class. Lap speeds for the top class, 250 Formula E, are around the 115 mph mark; the record for karts being held by Nigel Smith in a time of 1 m 30.76s, at a speed of 116.10 mph. For the Grand Prix the full circuit is used but without the Woodcote chicane and the sight of half a dozen or more karts drifting through on to the Main Straight is one that is well worth seeing.

John Shaw, Secretary of the Cadwell Club and an RAC Scrutineer.

Peter Carter (left), Tony Temple (centre) and Ian Rushforth; the trio at the helm of the Central Kart Club.

Marshalls are an essential part of the kart racing scene ... turning out in all weathers.

The lap scoring team seen here in their lofty perch above the start line at Mallory Park.

First aid and emergency services are also an essential part of the scene.

Not the best way to end a race ... but the breakdown truck provides a very necessary service.

Derek Rodgers seen sticking to the left of the circuit as he negotiates the first left-hander leading to the Mountain.

Whilst we have mentioned only one or two individuals in our summary of the circuits used it should not be forgotten that, as in other forms of organised sport, there is a vast army of people working away behind the scenes to ensure the smooth running of meetings. The respective Club Secretaries will, prior to events, have to deal with the volume of paperwork associated with entries etc. The circuits have to be booked for the dates required, well in advance when using motor racing venues, and programmes have to be compiled and printed.

No race meeting could be held without the long-suffering, and often voluntary, marshalls. These people stand out in all sorts of weather conditions for very little, if any, reward. The lap scoring girls work frantically throughout the meeting recording the progress of every driver, usually in the company of the official time keepers. First aid and emergency services are a vital part of the racing scene and in many cases it is the local branch of the St. John Ambulance Association in attendance. For those drivers unlucky enough to encounter problems out on the track, a kart recovery service is also required and, here again, in most cases it is volunteers who provide the necessary service. The problems of recovering broken down karts is, of course, more difficult on a full motor racing circuit than it is on a shorter kart track but over the years a good system has evolved and problems are usually kept to a minimum and racing is not held up.

For the bigger events such as the Grand Prix then, as we said earlier, planning starts for the next year's event as soon as the current one is over. Once the date is ratified then advertising would start just after Christmas and regulations for competitors would be issued early in the year. For an event held in the summer, June or July, meetings with the event's sponsors would start in March when all aspects of the promotion would be discussed. About six weeks before an event like the Grand Prix press releases would be sent out and posters advertising the meeting sent to garages, pubs and hotels, accessory shops etc. Around 3000 would be distributed in total. Three or four weeks before the event a press day would be held at the circuit when members of the press would be invited to drive a kart. The idea is, of course, to generate as much pre-event publicity as possible.

Silverstone, the Grand Prix venue, is well geared to such prestige events and throughout the year all aspects of the promotions departments are kept in top gear. Circuit safety, catering, etc. are all being dealt with as a matter of routine. As with all motor racing circuits used by karts the special needs of these mini racers is taken care of such as the placing of straw bales around the unforgiving Armco. To name everyone involved in promoting and organising the sport would need much more space than is available in a volume of this size. It is true, though, that without that army of mainly voluntary workers, giving up much of their free time, the show would simply not go on.

Driving Impressions

In order to try and give you a closer look at the circuits used we asked three of the top drivers to put their thinking caps on and re-live a lap of their favourite circuit. Here is a description of each one corner-by-corner:

The 250 National British Champion, Derek Rodgers, has always had a liking for Cadwell Park with its many twists and turns placing extra demands on both kart and driver so we start with Derek's view of that circuit from the driving seat.

As he flashes past the commentary/timing box on the main straight he will have the Zip/Yamaha flat out in top, that's fifth gear, at around 135 mph. No backing off for the left handed sweep up Coppice as he aims for a late apex to get the best line for the next corner, the right hander at Charlies. Braking is not necessary as some speed will have been scrubbed off as he climbs towards Charlies. Down to fourth gear just before turning onto Park Straight, again looking for that late apex in order to make the straight as long as possible. Every yard counts if a fast lap is to be achieved.

As Derek hits the bottom of the dip he is back in fifth with his right foot hard down until the 100 yard marker board looms up. Then it's on the brakes ... hard ... and down to third for Park Corner, taken from the far left of the circuit, across the apex and just missing the grass! Exiting Park Corner the power has to be fed in just at the right time or it is too easy to induce some oversteer and end up in the rough, in a spin, literally. The right handed Chris Curve is then looming up and just before turning in Derek will have snatched fourth gear, drifting to the outside of the circuit. It's then quickly back up to fifth and as late as possible turn back across the track, a quick dab on the brakes, back down to fourth and just clip the concrete on the right. That should have put the outfit on the right-hand side of the tarmac ready for the left-hander into the Gooseneck. Derek just finds time for a quick burst on the throttle before going back on the brakes and downhill towards Mansfield Corner.

If the track is dry, no real problems are encountered, but on a wet day this corner will sort out the good from the not so good. Keeping to the right of the track downhill Derek is back on the brakes and selecting third gear. If he doesn't get it just right it is very easy to understeer straight off

into the grass. Not a very pleasant way to end your race! Getting it perfect, however, Derek enters the Club Circuit start/finish straight back up in fourth, accelerating hard and snatching top gear through the left-handed kink leading to the Mountain section. The Mountain is a very steep, short climb but before that point Derek will be on the brakes hard, down to third for the first left hander and turning in late. Keeping as far left as possible he will clip the apex at the foot of the climb as he powers up the hill. It is important to have a good line here for as the kart crests the rise it will leave the ground and Derek will be flying. Too far to the left and kart and driver may well be deposited in the rough, not to be recommended at high speed. Passing the pits complex Derek's wife, Gayle will most probably be stationed there, stopwatch in hand keeping a keen eye on hubbie's progress.

Derek meanwhile will have selected fourth gear and be heading rapidly for Hall Bends. This section, through the woods, is a right, left, right and Derek takes the first right still in fourth before lifting off and snatching third for the left-hander. As he takes the left-hander and then passes under the old footbridge Derek will aim to stay well over to the left of the track before braking hard for the tight hairpin. It's down to first gear for this one, with another late apex and plenty of wheelspin on leaving as the power is applied. The outfit will be forced over to the left of the circuit, Derek lining it all up for the short dash to Barn Corner. Third will have been engaged and its back to the brakes before turning in to the right hander. As Derek so nicely points out, "If I get that one wrong, the barn doors are usually open, so all is not lost!" Sliding out to the edge of the track again Derek will be back up to fourth with foot hard down as the main start/finish line looms up again. Into fifth gear and Derek will flash over that line to start another lap of 2¼ miles and if the timekeepers show anything around 1 minute 34 seconds then Derek is on lap record pace and probably leading the race!

For ex-British Champion in the Superkart Class, Chris Lambden, Donington Park has always been a favoured venue. As Chris says, the surface is good, safety run off areas are excellent and every corner of the track offers a different approach. To get the best out of a 250 Rotax, Donington calls for good clean, smooth lines if the driver is to produce a quick lap. So sit back, brace yourself and imagine you are at the wheel of Chris Lambden's Talasan sponsored Zip/Rotax in a flying lap of the Derbyshire track.

Crossing the start/finish line Chris will be in fourth gear, as the revs climb so fifth will be selected before he is on to the brakes for Redgate Corner. Braking point is somewhere around the

On the exit of the tight first-gear hairpin plenty of boot for the short dash to Barn Corner.

Having braked hard from about 135mph, Chris Lambden takes a tight line through the first right at Park Chicane.

end of the pit exit road and firm use of the middle pedal is called for to bring the speed down for the right-hander. Depending on the traffic situation and the tightness of his line, Chris may find he has to take second gear but ideally he will be in third, going in deep and wide, arcing across on the widest but smoothest path. On leaving Redgate it is then up through the gearbox into top (sixth) and sweeping down Craner Curves towards the very deceptive Old Hairpin. For this one Chris will take fourth, again with a wide sweeping line but as before, if traffic means he is caught tight, it will be down one, to third. The track then goes left twice, through Coppice and onto McCleans with Chris back up to fifth. As McCleans looms up the gearbox is in use again as third is selected, feeding the power in as the outfit twitches over the slight bump on the apex. As he slides out to the kerbing its back up to fourth with just time to snatch fifth briefly but then its braking time again and down the box to third for the double apex Coppice. A smooth fast exit is required here to get onto the straight as cleanly and as quickly as possible.

Under the Dunlop Bridge, and Chris will be in top but already looming up large is the Park

Up to third gear as Chris leaves the Chicane and enters the main straight.

Kurt Luby lifts a front wheel as he powers out of Lodge Corner at his favourite circuit, Oulton Park.

With Lodge in the background, Kurt approaches Deers Leap on his way to start another lap.

Chicane, and at 135 mph Chris is approaching rapidly. Braking points for this one vary; Chris chooses a spot just past the first advertising hoarding on the left-hand Armco, and each time just hopes that the advertiser hasn't changed! The chicane itself is taken in second gear, firstly flicking right then as he leaves to enter the start/finish straight he is up to third and heading for the start of another lap. Given a good passage Chris will have recorded a time of around 1 minute 13 seconds which even the likes of Barry Sheene and Randy Mamola will find hard to beat aboard their 750cc-powered Superbikes!

For the last of our three flying laps 21 year old double British Champion in the 125 class, Kurt Luby, chose Oulton Park as his favourite venue, its twists and turns calling for a high degree of skill and nerve.

After the start/finish line the first corner is Old Hall and Kurt will have the engine screaming at around 12000 rpm as he turns in. As he hits the bumps the revs drop, Kurt's vision goes blurred and he drops down a gear before accelerating hard, trying to avoid the big bump on the apex, yet attempting to exit the corner as quickly as possible. The track then smooths out a bit, the engine revs reach 12200, Kurt takes top gear approaching Cascades. The red and white painted kerbs look like mountains as the track drops downhill and for a fleeting moment Kurt feels that he is going off the end of the world! Just as quickly the track is back in view and sweeping left as Kurt turns in. The g-forces are incredible, vision is again blurred and the kart is twitching as if everything is stretched to the absolute limit. It's

then onto the brakes, hard, and then even harder as Kurt tries to keep the outfit on something like the right line for the right-hander coming up. As third is selected the back end tries to go its own way as Kurt fights to keep the whole outfit on the kerb line. Back up to fourth and vision is clear again as Kurt is looking up Clay Hill snatching fifth as he approaches the brow, hugging the kerb on the left as if his life depended on it! Kurt has to push himself physically down into the seat as the whole thing takes off over the hill. At the same spot he will instinctively duck his head as he goes under the bridge, feeling that if he doesn't he won't have a head to duck on the other side. The engine revs up like a jet, sixth is selected and as the kart lands again it flicks over to the right. That was why Kurt was hanging on to the kerb as though his life depended on it!

Two corners further on is Druids but from this point Kurt is already planning his approach to that one, flat out in top trying to make it all as smooth as possible, at the same time using every inch of the track. The kart is sliding away from Kurt all the time and its a constant battle to keep control, forcing himself to clip the inside kerbs and not the outside as the corner before Druids is a double apex. Incredible g-forces return, the back of the kart tries once more to overtake the front but by now Kurt is committed, there is no turning back! This is really the point when confidence in his own ability and his equipment is most critical, for after hanging on for what seems ages the track straightens up and Kurt has time ... just ... to snatch a breather.

Under the Dunlop Bridge and the head goes

down again, mustn't lose his head twice in one lap, the revs rise to about 12000 and more. Lodge Corner is now in sight and Kurt's eyes are firmly fixed on his braking point, his thoughts centred on whether he dare knock a foot off it, but realising that if he does he simply won't make it. The right foot goes on the brakes, down one gear and the back end starts to slide, down two and track disappears to the right. Down the box again and the power is back on with the kart becoming very light and at an angle of 45 degrees to the road. Kurt finds himself sliding downhill on the bad adverse camber changing up to fourth as he hits the dip and climbs up Deers Leap. Hugging the left hand side of the track and looking up at the

Marshalls post the start/finish line is in sight again as he drifts to the right brushing the Armco. Under the bridge and up the box to sixth Kurt is then flat out as he flashes over the line to begin another hair raising, but quick lap.

Just to give you some indication of the time factor and speeds involved it is interesting to note that Derek Rodgers will complete a flying lap of Cadwell in about the same time as it would take you to read about it from the comfort of your armchair. And we shouldn't think your favourite chair twitches as much as Derek's Zip/Yamaha!

4 The Class Structure

In Britain karting is split into two main categories: a) the 100cc and 135cc direct drive classes which are allowed to compete on the short specialist kart tracks and;
b) the classes with which we are mainly concerned, that is, the gearbox categories which compete on both short and long circuits.

Before we get into the main theme of the book, the gearbox classes on long circuits, we will look briefly at the non-gearbox classes and what they can offer the competitor. It is a fact that of the 3500 licence holders in this country about 90% of them compete only on short circuits with a large proportion being in the non-gearbox category. That category is further split into Junior and Senior ranks with a class to suit most tastes and, more importantly, most pockets. At Junior level there are three classes: Junior Booster; Junior Britain; and Junior International.

The **Junior Booster Class** was new for 1984 and competitors can enter at the age of ten. New regulations were formulated by the RAC to come into force at the beginning of 1984 with the accent on bringing in a low cost class for the younger driver. Restrictions are placed on tuning, a complete rolling chassis must cost no more than £385 and the mandatory Bridgestone tyres have a maximum size. Front and side body panels are allowed so the karts will take on a more attractive appearance and go some way to matching their larger gearbox counterparts.

The next Junior class is **100 Junior Britain**. Here again maximum price rules are in force and, as its name implies, the chassis must be commercially produced in Britain. The current RAC Yearbook lists all the permitted engines and gives maximum prices for both engines and chassis. As per the 1984 regulations one could in

theory start in this class for a little under £700.

If you wish to go one better and enter world class competition then perhaps **Junior International** is the class you should be looking at. As with all international classes this one is run to CIK regulations and is the class in which all top level Junior karting takes place.

By the time one reaches the ripe old age of 16, a move up to the senior equivalents of the foregoing classes is necessary. The first of these is the **100 Britain** class for which, apart from an increase in the weight limits, all aspects of the class are the same as for its junior counterpart. Numerically the best supported class is the **100 National** category and again the only significant difference between this one and the junior counterpart is the increase in weight limits. This is an excellent class to really develop your racing skills and learn the art of kart control with some fierce competition being encountered.

The pinnacle of non-gearbox racing is either 100cc or 135cc **International** and this is where all the top class world events come into the reckoning. A decline in the 100cc class coupled with the introduction of the 135cc category has meant that the World Title is now competed for at the higher engine capacity level. There are moves within the sport to bring about a revival of the 100cc International, the view of many being that the 135cc class has not taken off in the way that it was hoped. International classes are governed by the CIK and, as with most forms of world level motor sport, the restrictions on equipment and tuning are much less severe than at national level.

Before we move on to the gearbox classes it should be noted that, whilst minimum age limits are in force, there is no upper age limit so one can continue to race until the pension book is issued.

1984 saw the introduction of the Junior Booster Class.

An example of Junior Britain.

The top class of Junior karting, run to CIK regulations.

The first of the Senior classes — 100 Britain.

The 100 National Class. Always well supported and, as you can see, spectacular.

100 International, the pinnacle of non-gearbox karting until the introduction of the 135cc class. It is hoped that the class will make a comeback at world level.

Whilst on the subject of age, in addition to the RAC classes covered there is a very active schools karting set-up throughout the country with the National Association of Schools Karting looking after the interests of children. An excellent publication has recently appeared through the Castrol Educational Division and gives a great deal of advice and information about all aspects of Schools Karting from forming a club to building and racing a kart. So there's a thought, if your teacher is not yet into karts and you would like him to be, in order that you might be, then the book gives an excellent introduction and will guide you through the complexities of it all.

Now we will move on to the gearbox classes which, as mentioned do operate on both types of circuit. The only noticeable difference will probably be a lack of fibreglass fairings and wings on the short circuit variety with a need for different gearing on the short circuits. Many drivers do in fact find the time to compete on both types of track and are just as competent on either. Taking the gearbox classes in order of engine capacity we will first look at the youngest of the long circuit categories!

125 National

This class has only been around the long circuits for the last six years or so but rapidly proved a very popular class. The RAC Blue Book lists all the accepted engines and, as with all classes, lists all the technical requirements. With an engine of 125cc maximum capacity driven through a gearbox with a maximum of seven ratios, the class has over the last few years overtaken all other categories in driver popularity. Regular entries of 60 and more provide some marvellous close racing with up to a dozen of the top drivers being capable of winning races. As with all gearbox classes, four wheel braking is allowed, unlike the

non-gearbox classes which have their stopping power on the rear wheels only. A wide variety of chassis is also evident in the 125 class and 1984 saw the introduction of an alternative engine in the shape of the Italian Minarelli. Apart from a brief spell with such exotic power plants as the Kawasaki the majority of drivers stick with the Austrian Rotax.

210 National

This class has been around in this country almost from the word go, it being the oldest gearbox class. It has in recent years suffered from a drop in the number of active participants but still provides some good racing at not too high a cost. The Villiers engine upon which the class is based is getting rather long-in-the-tooth, though Aubrey Upton has done a great deal to maintain a supply of parts as the original Villiers components become more and more difficult to locate. A maximum of four gears is allowed in this class and some relatively inexpensive equipment can be found. The class has stuck to the old bare look for a number of years with the fibreglass fad only just beginning to catch on. For the faster circuits such as Silverstone though, some fine examples of front fairings have been wheeled out; many years ago Dud Moseley unveiled a fully bodied Villiers outfit and campaigned it with some success.

250 National Class

This class is restricted to single-cylinder power units of 250cc with a maximum of five gears. Before the advent of the twin-cylinder engines this class was the top class of karting but has been in serious decline over the last few years. However, a newcomer to the sport, Yorkshireman Adrian Lumb, took the bull by the horns, so to speak, and mainly through his efforts of a couple of years ago revitalised the class and increased entries almost threefold. The idea was basically a simple one, as

135 International produces some spectacular close racing at world level.

Schools karting produces some rather unusual designs compared to the commercially marketed karts.

A further example of a school prepared outfit.

most good ideas are; Adrian persuaded a good number of drivers to dip into their own pockets and put cash into a central fund. The total was then split into prize money over a five-round series with start money guaranteed. It worked, and although Adrian has now slipped away from active involvement in karting the class is thriving once more and producing some excellent competition. From 1 March 1985 water-cooled engines will be eligible. It will be interesting to see how the class develops as a result of this.

250 Formula E

This is the final class in long circuit racing and is karting's answer to Formula 1. Since the mid-seventies when Sidney Taylor registered the name Superkart that name has been the one generally used when referring to this class. This is the ultimate in gearbox and long circuit karting and is run to International rules formulated by the CIK. Either air- or water-cooled engines are allowed although, since the introduction of the water-cooled Austrian Rotax, the majority of drivers discovered that to remain competitive this was the engine to have rather than the air-cooled Yamaha twin.

Aerodynamics have begun to play an important part in the class and in that respect Martin Hines has done a lot to develop the art of working with fibreglass. Wind tunnels and Formula 1 experts have also played a part in producing the best in wind-cheating designs. For spectacle and sheer speed it is difficult to imagine a more exciting branch of motor racing. Speeds of up to 140mph are attained on the faster circuits and to witness a full grid of Superkarts straining at

A long circuit version of 125 National, probably the most popular class of kart on motor racing circuits.

the bit waiting for the green light is a sight not to be missed. Once seen you will, we are sure, want more.

Inevitably with increased technology there has been a marked increase in costs at this level resulting in a drop in the number of active participants. When compared with other forms of motor racing karting, however, even at the top level, Superkarts still offer fantastic value for money and is perhaps the nearest thing to formula racing at a fraction of the cost.

To cover all the technical regulations would require much more space than is available so we have been able to give only a brief outline of what it is all about. Either your local club or the RAC will be only too pleased to offer sound advice should you want to look further into the various classes and it's almost certain that somewhere within karting's structure you will find what you want at a price you can afford.

Although suffering from a decline in entries, the 210 class can still offer relatively cheap racing.

The single-cylinder 250 National Class offers keen competition with much improved entries.

The premier class in gearbox karting, 250 Formula E. Colourful and highly spectacular, the karts are capable of speeds of up to 140mph.

5 Equipment

To attempt to cover every item of equipment necessary in order to go long circuit kart racing would require far more space than is available within this volume. What we will attempt to do however is give you some idea of the basics involved in the hope that your understanding of the sport will be enhanced. Any of the drivers involved will be willing to talk to you about any aspect about which you may be unclear, and in talking to those drivers you will also begin to realize just how much of an individual's sport karting has become.

Almost without exception each driver has his own ideas on how to get the best from his machinery and over the years some very ingenious examples of individuality have made an impression on the sport. It is a fact, though, that the 'bush telegraph' works quite well and it is amazing how quickly one driver's 'brilliant' idea soon becomes the accepted way for the majority.

The Chassis

To put it in the most simple terms a kart chassis has to be designed in such a way that it has provision for mounting all the essential component parts. Wheels, a driver's seat, engine, steering gear and fuel tank must all come into the overall picture when first starting on the drawing board. Over the last fifteen years or so the basic design of a kart chassis has remained fairly stable with no great changes having taken place.

There are now only a handful of manufacturers involved in the production of chassis compared to the large number in existence during the early sixties. Without exception a frame or chassis is of welded construction and formed from aircraft specification Chrome Moly tubing. Usually of 14

gauge and 1⅛ inch diameter it is strong enough to withstand the extreme stresses of racing yet has sufficient flex to allow the whole outfit to absorb movement. A kart has no suspension, indeed none is allowed under the regulations, so the frame is built to flex. Coupled with the 'give' in the tyres the flexing effect provides the suspension.

Fortunately most kart chassis are much easier to set up than a competition car. As we have just said there is no suspension, so critical settings for ride height, etc. are not required. Recently one or two manufacturers, notably Dino and Spyda, have incorporated adjustable steering geometry in their chassis but even this does not present too many problems when it comes to making adjustments for a particular track. Obviously, a brand new chassis should be straight and true and the key word to apply in that respect is that all things should be 'equal'. This applies to angles, lengths, diameters and circumferences on one side of the frame when compared to the opposite side. Castor and chamber angles, king pin inclination, axle measurements, tyre diameters, wheelbase and so on all come into the equation when setting up a chassis. Any chassis, regardless of make, must be 'square' if it is to perform satisfactorily and this basic requirement is best checked with the rear axle fitted in its carriers. The first measurement to be taken is the distance which the rear axle protrudes at each side of the chassis side members. The distance should of course be the same on each side. Next measure the distance from each front king pin to the back axle, again this should be the same. To determine finally if a chassis is square, take a measurement from each king pin diagonally to the rear axle. If each set of measurements has proved to be equal then the frame can be safely regarded as correct. Whilst everyone may be a perfectionist at heart, perfection is rarely achieved but any differences of more than 2 mm should be further investigated. A check of the type just described can be carried out on any flat surface of suitable size, if the better half doesn't mind too much the kitchen table will do nicely!

The criterion of squareness applies to any type of chassis, be it the ubiquitous 'waisted' Zip or the recently introduced A-frame from Phoenix Karts. The latter type of frame is not totally new to karting having been tried many moons ago by Zips, but with little success. At that time limitations on the type and quality of tyres, coupled with the non-availability of a suitable high quality tubing did nothing to help development and for some time the A-frame disappeared from the scene. Recent improvements in both rubber and tubing, however, have prompted Jim and Kurt Luby to tackle the A-frame once more, and Kurt has successfully campaigned one in the 125cc class on both long and short circuits.

If one takes the Zip chassis as being the standard work then those which vary from that standard include, in addition to the Phoenix, the Danish manufactured Dino and the Suffolk produced Spyda of Harry Webb and Ian Rushforth. Ed Duckett did until recently import the Dino but has now branched out on his own in producing a Dino look-alike, the EDR. In the case of the Dino and Spyda the chief differences are to be found in the steering geometry, it being adjustable for castor in the case of the Dino and both castor and camber in relation to the Spyda. For those of you well acquainted with such technical terms no further explanation is necessary but for those of you taking an interest for the first time a little more knowledge will perhaps be welcome.

In simple terms, castor is the angle at which the king pins lean back from the vertical. The basic effects are that with a greater angle, or more castor, the inside front wheel will tend to lift more although there will be more apparent grip at the front in relation to the rear when travelling straight ahead. The penalty will be more tyre wear. A lesser degree of inclination from the vertical will produce the opposite effect giving less lifting of the front wheel, probably an element of understeer, less grip but less tyre wear and lighter steering. On karts with non-adjustable castor the angle can vary from 10 to 18 degrees whilst with the more sophisticated, adjustable, variety any setting between those figures can be achieved.

The term camber applies to the amount by which the front wheels lean inwards when in the straight ahead position. This is incorporated to give the best 'wear' pattern across the full tyre tread under cornering loads and is obviously the same angle as that which the stub axles make with the horizontal. Unless a stub axle has been damaged then it follows that correct kingpin inclination implies correct camber angle. It may all sound rather complicated but at the moment most kart chassis do not have an adjustment facility built in so not too many people have to get involved in deciding the best settings.

After continuous use most chassis will start to get 'tired' and if any major surgery is deemed necessary then it is best left to the manufacturer. He will after all have all the jigs and equipment, not to mention experience, to put it right. Often though, a slightly twisted chassis, perhaps the result of a minor shunt whilst racing, can be straightened sufficiently to enable one to continue racing. The method might be a bit primitive but it can work and save an early retirement. Many of the knocks a kart takes can result in one of the sides being slightly higher at the front than the other. If that is the case the kart will, when the driver's grip is relaxed, veer off the straight and narrow instead of continuing in a straight line. Provided the kart can be placed on a flat surface with the driver seated normally a reasonable repair operation can be carried out. One corner will feel 'lighter' than the other when lifted so an assistant is required to lift each corner in turn to determine which is the lighter side. The kart will then have to be raised off the ground with some solid support under the king pin area on the heavy side. By exerting pressure of weight it is possible to bend the chassis so as to bring it back to something like square in the horizontal plane. Obviously, much more elegant methods are available in the workshop and are to be recommended but the system described will give reasonable results and probably enable you to get a full day's racing instead of half a day. Often even a new chassis can be improved by very careful attention to detail when building for there are bound to be slight discrepancies due to volume production.

Chassis are, of course, like all kart equipment, clearly defined in the current RAC and CIK technical regulations so if you are not sure about anything ask someone who should know before going ahead with your ideas.

Wheels, Tyres and Brakes

Tyres have always played a very important part in motor racing and karting has been no exception. As speeds have increased then so has the demand for better and better tyres. One of the most significant events in kart tyre technology was the introduction of Japanese Bridgestones to the sport in 1977. Martin Hines of Zip Karts played a major role in bringing Bridgestone into karting and has continued to work closely with that company in the development of new rubber for karting use.

All the household names in tyre production — Goodyear, Dunlop, Michelin and Pirelli — have played a part in kart tyre production, but in recent years, especially on the long circuit scene, Bridgestone have dominated. Both Dunlop and Pirelli are beginning to make a comeback into the gearbox world of karts and both brands are in regular use by a number of drivers. Ed Duckett of EDR has had success with Dunlops through the driving of Steve Styrin whilst Kurt Luby has found his Pirelli rubber working well too.

When you consider that the maximum width of a rear kart tyre is around seven inches then you will realise that the construction of that tyre has to be of the highest quality. Tyres have always been the subject of much discussion and even now many believe that with present day speeds the current crop of rubber is not up to the demands of karting on long circuits. There is no doubt that races have been lost through tyres crying 'enough'. Leaving the political arguments aside, just two types of tyre are needed for kart racing; a treaded variety for wet weather use, and a slick type for dry weather. The only stipulations in the regulations regarding tyres for long circuits refer to a maximum size and a maximum price.

New tyres should never be simply placed on the rim, inflated, and expected to work adequately. Damage will almost certainly be caused and a few simple steps should be taken to help eliminate the possible failure of one or more tyres. Always scrub in tyres before using them at racing speeds. Increase speed gradually to bring them up to working temperatures. Tyres of any type, road or racing, are designed to work at certain pressures but here again drivers do show preferences for higher or lower pressures in an attempt to obtain the maximum performance from their rubber.

At the start of the 1984 season some form of tyre bead retainer became compulsory for long circuit use and in most cases this has been incorporated into wheel design and construction over the preceeding eighteen months in readiness for the new regulation.

The majority of kart wheels are either die-cast or spun alloy. A die-cast wheel offers considerable accuracy and ease of assembly which is almost impossible to get with a spun alloy type. Coming more into the karting arena in recent years has been the Minilite brand of wheel, with much research having come from the company's involvement in the world of Rallying. Balancing of wheels has become much more important with the increase in speeds and, usually, self-adhesive balance weights are used with portable wheel balancing equipment gracing many a pit area nowadays.

Part of the large stock of aircraft specification tubing used in the making of Zip karts.

The early stages of kart construction.

The Dino Front end assembly includes provision for adjusting castor. Also shown is the inboard position of the front brake disc.

The Spyda chassis allows adjustments in both castor and camber angles.

The component parts of a rear axle assembly.

Adjustable wheelbase is another feature of the Rushforth/ Webb produced Spyda chassis.

Having satisfied yourself that the chassis is square, the time consuming task of assembly can begin.

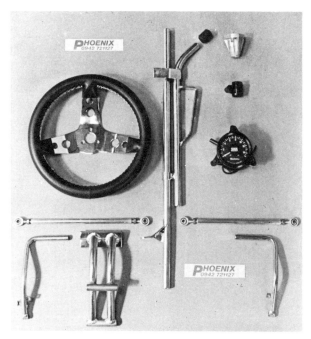

Essential component parts of the steering gear, together with all necessary foot pedals.

A batch of bare Zip frames waiting to be paint sprayed.

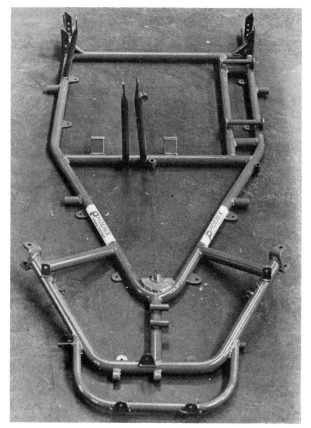

A Phoenix 125 class 'A' frame.

A jig such as this is used in the construction of a kart and will be needed should any major surgery be necessary.

A set of treaded tyres for wet weather use.

Slick tyres for use in dry conditions.

Some of the possible causes of races being lost. Look after your tyres!

The braking system on karts has evolved from a simple cable operated drum to the present sophisticated hydraulic disc variety. As in so many areas, most of the systems in use have been developed from those instigated by Zip Karts and operate in a conventional way. That is by displacing fluid from a master cylinder through pipes to a caliper, hence bringing the pads into contact with the disc. Evolution has inevitably brought changes and some current systems utilise the type seen on cars, i.e. with a fluid reservoir and self-adjusting brakes. The regulations state that karts in the gearbox classes (and that applies to all long circuit racing) must have brakes which operate on all four wheels. There is a preference, also for independent systems front and rear. The discs themselves have not changed too much although high quality Meonite is now used extensively in their production. Brake hoses which used to be of high pressure plastic are now more likely to be of the steel braided type such as Aeroquip. Brakes should always be kept in first class condition and checks should be made of all hoses to ensure no leaks are present in addition to checking all connections throughout the system. Discs should run true and straight, and pads should be regularly checked for wear.

Engines

Such has been the development of engines used in karting, with the exception of the 210 class, that many drivers feel that a 250cc Rotax, for example, is of adequate power straight from the box without further tuning. We will therefore confine our attentions to the types of power unit used in long circuit karting rather than make any attempt to determine what makes one quicker than another by investigation of individuals' tuning methods. The 210 National class utilises mostly, modern-day replicas of the Villiers 9 E engine/gearbox unit with four gears. The engine was designed shortly after the war for low-power applications so it is not too surprising that many people hold the view that in increasing its capacity from the original 196cc to its karting size of 210cc and increasing its operating speeds dramatically, too much was being asked. The class has always been in danger of extinction due to the shortage of genuine Villiers spares and it is due largely to one man, Aubrey Upton, that a supply of parts has been maintained. Aubrey, from his Fieldhouse Engineering business, has produced every conceivable part necessary from crankshafts to gearbox cogs. For many years the mainstay of British gearbox karting, the 210 class has suffered in recent years with a drop in numbers. Perhaps that has been due in part to the shortage of engines and spares although the view

is held in some quarters that the present day replica engines could go on pretty much forever.

The next class in terms of engine size is the 125 National category and this one is the boom class. Since first being allowed on to long circuits towards the end of the seventies a couple of engines have dominated the class. Initially it was the Yamaha of Steve Elmore which carried off all the honours, with Brian Hill also sharing in the glory with the more exotic Kawasaki 125 version. It wasn't long though before the Austrian Rotax make appeared on the gearbox scene and almost immediately began winning. The Rotax 124 model of 125cc has been developed from a motorcycle or snowmobile unit and will give around 30 bhp and rev freely up to 12500/13000 rpm. Almost every modern innovation has been incorporated in the Austrian product including a Nikasil coating on the cylinder similar to

A selection of wheels including one of the Minilite variety (top).

A cross section of the Minilite wheel showing tyre bead retaining facility.

A variation in wheel design, the Dino one piece example.

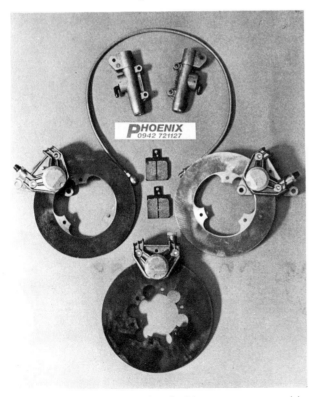

The component parts of a kart braking system, as used by Phoenix.

that used on the Le Mans winning Porches and road going BMW motorcycles.

The 125 class, during the last couple of years, has produced some excellent entertainment and the little Rotax engine driving through a six-speed gearbox has played its part to the full. There is, however, to be a challenger to its supremacy in the shape of a new engine to karting in this country; the 125 Minarelli from Italy. Through their Phoenix Karts business, Jim and Kurt Luby are importing this engine.

Kurt used the engine at the first meeting of 1984 at Cadwell and won in style. He returned to the same venue in September 1984 and scored his second victory with the new engine. The signs are that the 125 class is about to enter a period of very keen competition. Bob Clowes has also been instrumental in bringing about a surge of popularity for a 125 class using reed valve and piston timed motors such as Honda and Yamaha produce. This engine offers the chance to go racing at reduced cost and has proved quick and reliable.

The engines used in the 250 National class must, by the rules of the sport, be of single-cylinder type with a maximum of five gears. Spanish engines such as the Bultaco used to dominate this class as far as power was concerned but gradually the Japanese took over just as they have done in the motor cycle world. The YZ250G air-cooled engine has become the driving force in this class, a unit developed from a motor cross machine and proving to be very successful in karting.

As from 1st March 1985 water-cooled engines have been eligible for use in this class.

The mention of water-cooling brings us to the summit of long circuit karting and that is the 250 Formula E class, or Superkarts as they have become widely known in recent years. Since the beginning of 1981 the engine to use in this class has, without doubt, been another product from the Austrian Rotax factory, the model 256. This is a twin-cylinder, water-cooled, rotary valve engine which, revving to 12500 rpm and producing around 70 bhp, is capable of propelling a Superkart at 140 mph. The twin, in-line cylinder, configuration is not entirely new, Kawasaki having pioneered the set-up in their successful road racing machinery. Rotax however were able to turn the idea into a production model at reasonable cost. The basic layout of the engine has the two cylinders, one behind the other, both crankshafts being joined by a pair of tandem gears, one at the end of each crankshaft. The rear cylinder incorporates a further toothed gear which drives directly onto the clutch drum, hence through to the gearbox. The clutch gave problems, but a beefier assembly introduced in

An example of the Villiers 9E type of engine used in the oldest class; the 210 National.

An alternative brake system as used on the 1983 Sisley Cobra, a twin caliper rear set-up.

The Rotax 125cc which has dominated the class over the last few years.

the last eighteen months seems to have gone a long way to solving that problem. In an attempt to obtain the best possible power performance from this unit the use of dynomometers has increased although as yet only a few people in karting have access to such equipment.

Ignition

Before any engine will run it does, of course, need ignition, and probably the most important single piece of equipment on a racing kart engine is the ignition system. Advances through the years have produced the modern transistorised set-up which is capable of producing a consistent spark of a relatively high voltage at speed in excess of 20000 rpm. Most systems used in karting are self-induced, i.e. no external power source is needed; a rotating magnet produces an electrical current through a series of transistors. Because of the varying requirements of the engine at different rpm provision is made to advance or retard the time at which the spark occurs. The one drawback to this system is that it does require energy (albeit a small amount) to turn the rotor against the resistance of the magnetic pole. Recently moves have been made to overcome this by introducing a battery-powered system.

Carburation

Modern karts, without exception, carry a fuel tank which is situated lower than the carburettor. The problem arises in pumping the fuel from the tank to the carburettor, and many different types of pump have been tried. One method is to use a diaphragm pulse type pump which is activated by the alternating pressures created within the crankcase. Connections are made by a capillary tube, usually into the crankcase. The level of fuel is controlled by using cut-off valves in the carburettor, various sizes of which are used in order to meter the correct flow of fuel. An alternative method of supplying fuel from the tank is to use a mechanical type of pump activated by a cam fitted to the rear axle. Where a mechanical pump is fitted the system usually incorporates a fuel resistor to cut down the pressure at which the fuel is supplied. This is adjustable and is used as a means of obtaining the correct supply. So, next time you see a driver sitting in his outfit and being gently rolled back and forth it is simply to operate the pump cam on the axle and not intended to put him to sleep!

As in most forms of motor racing, individuals in karting have shown great ingenuity in further adapting one, or even both, of the systems. Having achieved a required flow of fuel to the carburettor the subsequent attention to that area

A likely challenger to the Rotax 125. The Italian Minarelli.

The Honda engine used in the 125 P & R class.

The Minarelli variety of 125 P & R engine.

The Yamaha as used in the 250 National class.

The Austrian Rotax Model 256. The peak in engine power for the 250 Formula E class.

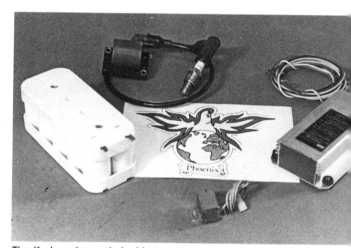

The Krober electronic ignition system as used on the 125 of Kurt Luby.

Dynamometers have played an increased role in engine preparation. This example is based at Zip's premises.

Carburation plays a critical role in kart preparation but exhausts can often be a case of trial and error deep into the realms of physics.

There is a good selection of lubricants available for the care of the kart's working parts.

is considered by many to be the most critical one can give to a kart. The variables obtained from a carburettor, a precision engineered unit, are many and complex. Atmospheric conditions can further change things substantially. Thus, a great deal of effort goes into the tuning of carburettors, both in the workshop and at the track side.

The Drive Train

Being motor-cycle based, all kart engines drive through an integral gearbox by means of a toothed sprocket and chain to the back axle. The important thing to ensure is that engine sprocket and back axle sprocket are perfectly aligned so as to reduce the possibility of throwing a chain. By changing the size of the sprockets one can, of course, change the gearing available and in that respect once more the individuality of karting comes to the fore with drivers having different ideas on what is best for a certain circuit. Whatever you do make sure that the sprockets are kept in good condition and are well lubricated.

Bodywork

The world of aerodynamics has become increasingly evident in long circuit karting in recent years. At first it was all very much trial and error and although forms of bodywork were to be seen many years ago it was open to debate as to

A Superkart with conventional fibreglass bodywork.

The latest fully-clothed example from the Zip camp.

The standard variety of bodywork as used on the Phoenix 125.

A selection of racing clothing available from Zip Karts.

A good quality leather suit is desirable, together with boots and gloves. A suit of waterproof material is a must for wet weather.

Frequently used in karting, the whirly visor will help towards clearer vision in the wet.

There are a number of top quality helmets available and it is wise to get the best you can afford.

All kart classes are governed by weight regulations and the scales play an important part on race day.

A familiar face around the circuits, RAC scrutineer and CIK representative, Ron Brassey. His job is to see that you comply with the regulations.

whether they were successful or just nice to look at. However, that man Martin Hines, again, has been very much involved in producing a range of fibre glass bolt-on goodies. With the help of that celebrated Formula One designer, Harvey Postlethwaite, wind tunnels have been extensively used to develop front nose cones, side tanks and rear wings culminating in a full racing car type body adorning many a 250 Superkart on long circuits. Whether it all works or not is still debatable to some but if nothing else it certainly provides expanses of reasonably flat fibre glass on

53

which to advertise your sponsors; if you are lucky enough to have one.

Personal Clothing

Kart drivers, unlike car racers, are almost totally exposed to the elements and, therefore, the choice of good quality clothing is an important point to ponder. If finances will allow a top quality tailor-made leather racing suit is desirable along with the best you can afford in the form of gloves and boots. A good helmet is, of course, a must and will have to comply with the regulations in force at the time of use. When you stop to think that your head is the only one you're ever likely to have then it makes sense to protect it with a top-quality lid. For wet weather driving an oversuit of waterproof material is necessary and many drivers make use of a whirly visor rather than constantly having to wipe the conventional type.

From the foregoing you should have got a good idea of some of the wide range of components that make up a complete racing kart. If you are going racing yourself then everything you do will be controlled by the current regulations and there to see you do comply will be RAC appointed scrutineers. The basis on which they work is one of safety, not just yours but the safety of all competitors and spectators alike. Enjoy it all and remember, you are doing it for fun ... really.

6 Spectating and Photography

Spectating

Karting is very much a family affair, in many ways. A casual spectator will soon realise that each small paddock section is made up of the karter's family: father, mother, brothers, wife or girl friends, sons and daughters are all there to act in some capacity. Their role may be that of mechanic, dog's-body, tea maker or just morale booster. Even the children are there: tiny babies in push chairs, toddlers on small bikes, older boys and girls on mini motor bikes. Stop watches and clip boards are very much in evidence as at least one member of the family will be charting the progress of their man.

Karters themselves refer to the 'family of karting', and newcomers to the sport will soon feel themselves adopted by the family. As any family loves to invite guests into its home, so the karting family welcomes spectators into its midst. There is no need for the spectator to feel he has to stay on his side of the fence so to speak. The gates to the pit and paddock area are always open and admission is usually free, except at the more important, larger meetings where a small charge is made. You are encouraged to wander round to view at close quarters the racing karts and to chat to the drivers. Without their all encompassing helmets they are very human and will be more then happy to chat about their sport and answer questions. Perhaps the only exception to that would be if the driver and his team of mechanics are engaged in a race against time to repair the outfit before the next race. Very soon you will feel as involved as they are and next time you see them on the track you are cheering, not just another race number, but for a new found friend. Suddenly you are hooked; Castrol R is very addictive.

The racing season, as far as the motor racing circuits are concerned, starts at Cadwell Park usually on the last Sunday of February. Now, February is not the month to choose to go sunbathing, more often than not the Lincolnshire parkland is covered in snow. Nevertheless it is not a bad place to take your first interest in karting on long circuits provided you are well wrapped up against the cold east wind. Thick overcoats and wellingtons are certainly the 'in' thing at that time of the year. Once you have found your way to a suitable vantage point you will quickly warm to the occasion with your first sight of a full grid of karts making its way down to the start line on the Club circuit. Unlike most other forms of motor sport, karting does usually boast very full grids with up to fifty drivers taking part in each race. We hope that this book will attract new spectators to the race meetings and in the following pages we will try and give you some idea of what to expect at your first event. As we said in the previous chapter the motor racing circuits may well be familiar to you if you are already involved in car or motorbike racing. You will therefore probably have a favourite viewing spot to which you have become quite attached. What then can the spectator get for his admission money? Having bought a programme you will first notice the large number of entries and the very full programme of events during the day.

At most national meetings, an entry of between 150 and 200 is commonplace and, with each of the four classes represented, you can expect to see up to fifteen races including the finals. For an admission price of around £2, with access to the pits area usually free, that is exceptionally good value for a day's entertainment. Apart from the more prestigious events

A happy Nigel Smith and family after his success in the TV Series of 1983. Young Martin appears to be taking up the bottle at an early age!

Cadwell Park in February and the need often arises for boots and snow shovels before racing can commence.

Not the best way to go snow clearing!

So you know what is happening during the day, programmes are readily available at all meetings.

such as the Grand Prix at Silverstone your admission ticket will allow you almost completely free access to all parts of the circuit. Do remember, though, that motor racing in any form is dangerous, a fact of which you should be reminded by the warning notices posted around the circuit. Do be guided by the marshalls and stay away from any dangerous spots. If the marshalls tell you that access is not allowed to any part of the surrounding area, then don't go. Animals are not allowed at motor racing events, for obvious reasons; a stray dog on the circuit can be extremely dangerous. If you must take your pet with you then make sure it is left in a vehicle out of harm's way, but don't forget to allow it some ventilation if you do leave it in the car. It's much better and safer to leave animals at home and thereby enjoy a trouble free day at the races.

As we said earlier, all the circuits in regular use for kart events do have facilities both for those attending just for the day and for anyone wishing for a slightly longer visit and able to take a tent or

NOTICE
WARNING TO THE PUBLIC
MOTOR RACING IS
DANGEROUS

IT IS A CONDITION OF ADMISSION THAT ALL PERSONS HAVING ANY CONNECTION WITH THE PROMOTION AND/OR ORGANISATION AND/OR CONDUCT OF THE MEETING, INCLUDING THE OWNERS OF THE LAND AND THE DRIVERS AND OWNERS OF THE VEHICLES AND PASSENGERS IN THE VEHICLES ARE ABSOLVED FROM ALL LIABILITY ARISING OUT OF ACCIDENT CAUSING DAMAGE OR PERSONAL INJURY (WHETHER FATAL OR OTHERWISE) HOWSOEVER CAUSED TO SPECTATORS OR TICKET HOLDERS

Situated at various points around the circuit, these signs are there to be complied with.

A view of the mini town at Silverstone for the 1983 Grand Prix.

caravan. Ample space is available and, indeed, at most meetings you will soon notice that the area surrounding the paddock takes on the appearance of a mini town. Motor homes, converted coaches, caravans and tents are all used by drivers and officials.

One of the first things that you will need to become familiar with is the class structure. Four classes take part in long circuit events and are dealt with in more detail in a later chapter, but for the spectators who simply want to be able to identify which class is which a very simple and easy to spot system is used. Each class carries a different coloured number on a coloured plate, as follows:

125 Nationals; white numbers on green plates.
210 Nationals; white numbers on red plates.
250 Nationals; black numbers on white plates.
250 Formula E; black numbers on yellow plates.

Novices of any class who have not obtained the required signatures on their licence always show black plates with white numbers. Unless there is a very small entry in one particular class each class will have its own races but should two classes be run together the colour coding will enable you to sort out one from the other. In addition, karting has its own unique system of allocating special numbers or letters to its respective champions and title holders. In each class the winner of the RAC Long Circuit Championship is entitled to carry the number 1 for the following year. The winner of the Grand Prix at Silverstone is awarded the much sought after lettering GP and again those letters are carried by the respective class winners.

The top bracket of long circuit karting, the 250 Formula E or Superkarts, perhaps come out best in the letters and numbers game. As well as the two mentioned this class also competes for three other major titles each having a special plate to honour the winner. The European Championship winner is awarded the letter E to signify his place at the top of European karting and from 1983 the newly instigated World Series for Formula E has a red Number 1 proudly displayed on the winner's kart. There is one other much coveted special number plate for the Superkarts and that is the red Zero on a white plate. Since 1968 that has been competed for at the World Cup event at Heysham. Although it is won on a short circuit it is carried with much pride by the winner when racing on long circuits.

It is a sad fact that 1983 was the last year that the World Cup appeared at Heysham. From 1984, a new International was instituted to take place at Donington Park. Most of the top drivers in the 250 ranks are of the opinion that the red Zero was THE plate to win and one driver, Richard

The proud recipients of the number 1 plates at Oulton Park in 1981. Top: Alan Collard, Chris Lambden; bottom: Roy Wooldridge, John Newton.

Paul Elmore, first ever winner of the coveted GP plates in 1978.

Rob Kerkhoven displaying the E plate having won the European Championship in Sweden in 1981.

The winner of the last World Cup event to be held at Heysham in 1983, Richard Dean.

Two of the 125 class front runners, Roy Wooldridge and Kurt Luby about to pass novice driver no. 13!

Dean of Ripley, will go down in history as the last man to win the coveted plate at Heysham in '83.

Having got the numbers and letters game sorted out and armed with the days programme you will have noticed, as mentioned earlier, the large number of races. Usually, depending on the entry, each class will take part in at least two heats and a final. At National events the starting positions for the heats are decided by ballot. That always throws up some interesting start positions with the recognised quick drivers taking the luck of the draw and often having a middle or rear of the grid position. It does, however, make for some very entertaining racing with those faster drivers carving their way through the field to attain the highest finishing spot possible. Points are awarded for heat positions and it is usually the top thirty or sometimes forty points scorers who go through to the final direct. Depending on the number of entries it may be necessary to have an additional race, termed a qualifier, in which all those outside the required number of points will compete. Usually the first ten will go forward to the final taking a place at the back of the grid.

Before the karts actually start a race they are required to form up in a dummy grid formation. This is to allow them a full or part lap of the circuit behind a pace car before lining up correctly at the start line. When the starter is satisfied that all is as it should be the signal is given and the race is on.

That system of heats and finals is used at all national events on long circuits but the procedure for CIK controlled meetings does show some differences. At these events, such as the European Championship and the World Series, a system of timed practice is used. All competitors are required to complete laps against the clock. Each driver's fastest time is then used to determine in which of three or four groups he will be placed to contest the heats. The fastest driver overall will head Group A; the second fastest Group B, and so on. Each of the groups then come together and race against each other with points awarded to each driver depending on his finishing position. The winner will score no points with second place two, third place three and so on. At the end of the heats the points are totted up and the driver with the least number of points takes pole position for the first of two finals. The top forty points scorers will automatically go forward to that first 'pre-final' with the remainder taking part in a last chance qualifying race from which the first ten will form the rest of the grid. The finishing order of the pre-final will then become the starting order for the main final i.e. the winner will have pole position. It may sound very complicated but once the system is running it works well and is relatively easy to follow. By now it is hoped, you will know what you are looking at and how the systems work.

What else might take your interest?

One thing which does stand out in kart racing is the close-quarters dicing taking place between the drivers in almost every race. Rarely do you see one driver disappear into the distance never to be caught. It does happen, but usually the spectator is treated to some excellent racing with anything up to a dozen karts contesting the same piece of tarmac. If you pick your spot carefully you will be able to see the driver working at the controls in an effort to extract the last ounce of performance and gain an advantage over his rivals. Often a good spot is the slowest point of the circuit, such as the hairpin on Cadwells Club circuit, where you will see the feet moving from brake to accelerator, hands trying to get just the right amount of lock on the steering and then snatch a higher gear to accelerate up the hill and try to leave all challengers way behind. On long circuits a walk around the track will give you a much more general view of proceedings and allow you to see the driver at work on different sections,

The hairpin at Cadwell is a favourite spot for viewing the karts at close quarters.

all of which will call for a different approach. Although we have said that the bulk of material in this book is concentrated around the motor racing circuits we must not forget the excellent viewing available on the short purpose built kart tracks. Due to their very nature, being much shorter and compact, a more general picture can be had by being in just one place. Most of the track can be seen and you do not have to content yourself with just seeing your new found hero negotiating one corner as is sometimes the case on long circuits.

There is one further very important aspect of the racing scene which is necessary for the spectators and that is the commentary team. As far as the long circuits are concerned one man, Don Briggs, has become an almost permanent fixture in the commentary boxes at virtually all the venues in this country.

From his lofty viewpoint, usually adjacent to the start line, Don is a vital link between the

If based in one spot, a more general view can be obtained at most of the short specialist kart tracks.

racing and the viewers. Over the years he has acquired an in depth knowledge of long circuit racing and will attempt to keep you fully informed as to what is happening out there on the tarmac. Coupled with snippets of information about individual drivers, his commentary and after-race results service will help to give you, the spectator, an enjoyable day out. A vantage point close to a relayed commentary point will certainly add to your enjoyment and you should leave a more knowledgeable person, keen to get to the next event.

The bulk of equipment which has been used to take most of the photographs in this book, purchased over a number of years.

The voice of karting – Don Briggs. A regular commentator at long circuit events, Don is rarely lost for words as he keeps you informed of what is happening.

Photography

For a number of people motor racing in any form offers the opportunity to fulfil those long held dreams of emulating the top sports photographers in capturing the action on film. To give you some idea of what is and what is not possible through the lens the following pages will help to guide you in how to prepare yourself and your camera.

One of the things you will notice when you first attend a kart meeting on a motor racing circuit is the size of the kart. Measuring about seven feet in length, three feet wide and around three feet high, they travel at an incredible speed. So how do you set about capturing such an animal on film? Without the proper tools no job can be done really well so the first essential is to equip yourself with a good camera. For motor sport purposes and karting in particular you will really need to have, or be prepared to buy, a 35mm Single Lens Reflex type of camera. These are readily available and

Interesting shots such as this can be found around the paddock area. A stroll with camera at the ready can produce worthwhile results.

Using a shutter speed of 1/500th of a second enabled the flying bath tub to be frozen.

A shutter speed of around 1/250th was used to capture this Superkart on the exit of the Cadwell Club circuit hairpin.

62   *The start of a 250 National Grand Prix final at Silverstone showing a panoramic view.*

A perfect example of the panning technique using a shutter speed of 1/500th at an aperture of f4.

Reg Gange shows how to celebrate after his Grand Prix victory in 1982.

universally popular. Three types are obtainable: manual; auto/manual and fully automatic. Inevitably, the type you buy will depend on the amount of money you are prepared to spend. Compared to the cartridge type 110 and 126 type of camera, the SLR offers much more versatility and there is a huge range of lenses and other accessories available should you really want to go to town.

In view of the small size of a kart when compared to, say, a saloon or Formula Ford racing car the lens you use will have a big bearing on the results you can expect. To take pictures from the spectator side of the Armco, and that is where most people will be, a lens of around 300mm is almost essential. At some tracks such as Silverstone, where the spectators are that much further away from the track, even a 600mm lens will not necessarily fit the bill. With the wrong lens you will get a lot of track and other background scenery with little karts in the middle of your picture. On some tracks you may well be able to get close enough to the action to use a 135mm lens and that size will also prove useful elsewhere should your karting interest wane. The standard lens, usually one of 50mm, supplied with the camera will prove quite adequate for any candid camera work you might feel able to do around the pit and paddock area.

A camera of any type is of little use without a good supply of film and for sporting purposes such as karting a fast film is desirable. The speed of a film is measured by its ASA or DIN number and the higher the number the more sensitive the film will be to light. It follows therefore that a 'fast' film of 400 ASA will be the most useful when you are operating in poor light conditions and using a fast shutter speed of perhaps 1/250th of 1/500th of a second. Those exposure settings are of course essential if you want to 'freeze' a fast moving racing kart. If you intend taking pictures purely for

This unusual headgear of Derek Rodgers proved very useful during the often wet 1983 season, particularly at Cadwell!

The secret of capturing a sequence such as this is to be in the right place at the right time. It is essential to follow the action through the viewfinder all the way. The sequence was obtained with a camera/winder using a 300mm lens with a shutter speed of 1/500th at around f8. Don't do the natural thing and run ... stick with it! All the drivers involved in the incident walked away uninjured.

your own pleasure, or to show to your friends, then of the three basic types of film available it would be best to stick to either colour print film or colour transparency film. You will then be able to fill your album with nice colour photographs or, using slides from the transparency film, put on some interesting viewing for family and friends. You will, though, be faced with additional expense if you choose the latter as a viewer or projector will be required. The third type of film available is the good old black and white stuff and again if you are aspiring to having your pictures published in newspapers or magazines then that is the film you should go for. Having spent a lot of your hard earned cash on a good camera and, perhaps, a couple of extra lenses, don't spoil it all by being a miser where film is concerned. Film is comparatively cheap and when you point your camera at the subject remember that is likely to be the only chance you will get to record that particular happening. Next time will be too late.

Before setting out for the race meeting you will also need to equip yourself with an adequate carrying case or bag for all your gear. One that is stout enough to withstand a knock but not too heavy or bulky to be comfortably carried is what you should aim for. Finally pack a small brush for lens cleaning and some waterproof clothing ... it often rains on race days ... and you are ready for your first sortie.

You should be fully conversant with the equipment you have and be in no doubt as to how it all works. One of the best spots to try out your new found skill is the slowest part of the track you are visiting. That is usually the hairpin and most tracks have at least one such corner where the karts are travelling at their slowest. A good example of such a spot is the hairpin on the Club Circuit at Cadwell Park. Safely positioned in the stand overlooking that corner you are ideally situated to catch the action. Try to focus on a part

of the track and shoot when the kart is in that spot, providing you have everything set as it should be the results will soon come. You will probably be surprised yourself! In order to 'freeze' a kart in motion you will need to use a shutter speed of at least 1/500th of a second going up to 1/1000th if the kart's speed is appreciably higher. Another good spot to shoot a few frames is at the start line. Here you will have the karts moving almost directly towards you with the added bonus of being able to fill your viewfinder with a large group of twitching machines.

Having tried your luck with the karts at a slight angle or directly in front of you the next technique to master is that of 'panning'. A shutter speed of 1/125th or 1/250th of a second will be needed but good results will only come with practice. So be prepared for some failures. The best photographers suffer those from time to time. The knack of panning is to stand comfortably but with feet firmly on the ground in a position where the karts will pass in front of you. Pick up the kart through the lens as it approaches the spot and follow it through, pressing the shutter button as it reaches the pre-focused spot. Follow the kart through just as smoothly as you did on its approach and you will, with practice, get a good picture of a kart in focus but with the background blurred ... giving a good impression of speed. It all may sound rather complicated but as with most things the more practice you get the better you will become. Don't, as we said earlier, be afraid to use film, even the professionals don't make every frame count.

Finally, some good and interesting shots can be found around the paddock area and if you enjoy seeing others receive the spoils of victory then stick around for the end of meeting prize giving. That can often be a very lighthearted affair after the rigours of a hard day's racing, producing some good photographic moments. Whatever type of camera you have there is something of interest to be snapped, so enjoy yourself but do remember ... motor racing is dangerous; don't stray from the permitted spectator areas unless you have previously cleared the way with the Secretary of the Meeting and signed the indemnity form. We have only been able to give an outline of the needs of a karting photographer and you may well already be very proficient but for those beginners amongst you we hope we have given you the encouragement to get out there and have a go.

7 The Media

Whatever the sport, be it karting or karate, a means of transmitting information to both participants and spectators is an essential ingredient for the furtherance of that particular sport's activities. In most cases the method chosen is the written word in the form of a magazine or newspaper. You only have to look on the shelves of any town or city centre bookshop to realise that just about every leisure activity ever invented is catered for in that respect. Karting is no exception and is well catered for by two monthly magazines; *Karting Magazine* and *Kart and Superkart.*

Karting Magazine has been around as long as the sport itself, having first seen the light of day way back in 1959. It was the brainchild of Alan Burgess and stemmed from a tiny advert in *Autosport* which announced that a demonstration of karting was to take place at Brands Hatch racing circuit. Along with thousands of other curious people Alan attended that event at the Kent circuit and on seeing the karts for the first time was hooked. He almost immediately afterwards took steps to form the British Kart Club and followed that with his first attempt at publishing. The initial offering was not a lavish affair, the first issue was entitled the *Go Karter* and was a 24-page duplicated publication mainly aimed at the members of that newly formed club. Events moved fairly quickly after that and, using part of his children's clothes shop in Beckenham, plans were made to offer a magazine for sale to the general public. With the interest in karting as a sport rapidly growing it was not surprising that a number of others attempted to follow Alan's lead and the result was more magazines. Titles such as *Karting News and Record; Kart News;* and would you believe, *Kum Karting,* appeared on the scene. Their involvement was comparatively short

lived and gradually they all disappeared from the scene leaving *Karting Magazine* as the sole publication.

During the next twenty years, to 1979, the one publication attempted, with a good degree of success, to promote karting in all its forms and bring news, views and technical advice to those

Karting Magazine, which celebrated its 25th Anniversary in 1984, started by Alan Burgess in 1959 and now edited by his son, Mark.

interested enough to want to know. Then in January of 1979 a second magazine was launched. The Zip karts business of Mark and Martin Hines formed a new Company, Kart and Superkart Ltd and began publishing a monthly with that title. Perhaps a little more glossy in appearance than *Karting* it offered an alternative in views and opinions and fairly quickly became established alongside *Karting.* Karters seem to be a breed which needs information and since '79 they have been well catered for through having the two publications, both offering a wide range of topics within their pages in addition to being a platform for individual's views. With the total number of kart licence holders currently around the 3500 mark potential sales of such specialist publications is to some extent limited although the need for them is beyond question. In addition to the two magazines dealing solely with karting matters the national weekly *Motoring News* also offers regular race reports throughout the season with the occasional news item when space permits. In most cases the national dailies take little interest in karting except during the build up to the Kart Grand Prix. As the *Daily Express* is involved in part sponsorship of that event then it is to be expected that in the weeks prior to the event

coverage will be given. A post-race report is also featured in the *Daily Express* on the Monday morning after the event. Sadly that is as much as one can expect from the national media outlets; karting hasn't yet reached the position of saturation coverage as in cricket and football, for instance. Generally speaking, those inside karting provide their own publicity, usually through part time contributors of race reports, news items, technical articles and photographs.

Moving from the written word to the visual coverage of karting events, television has, over recent years, shown an encouraging interest. Regional TV companies have from time-to-time shown items on the sport mainly from their own area but in November of 1980 a breakthrough came with some nationwide transmissions. Nick Brittan, himself once a kart driver, was the promoter of a specially staged 100 cc event held at Rye House stadium in Hertfordshire. It was a meeting built entirely around television and was screened on ITV's World of Sport. The result of that meeting was encouraging, but the repeat performance planned for the following year ran into problems and Nick Brittan then switched his attentions to the gearbox scene and the Superkarts. Donington Park was the venue in October

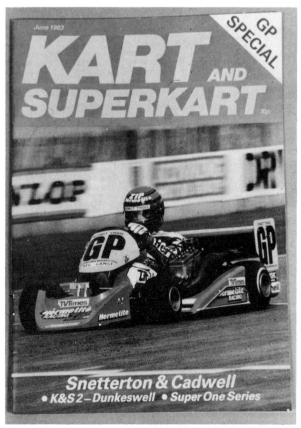

An alternative view of the sport is shown in a magazine launched by Mark and Martin Hines at the beginning of 1979.

Nick Brittan, former racing driver and successful promotor of karting TV, is seen discussing the filming of an event at Donington.

Essential BBC equipment in position ready to record the event at Donington in October 1981.

From a position overlooking the Park Chicane, a TV cameraman prepares to record the action.

FSO Cars' involvement in TV meetings can be clearly seen on the electronic scoreboard at Donington.

The most likely view from the camera position at Park Chicane — the Dunlop footbridge at Donington.

After a successful TV meeting the prettiest Superkart driver, Carolynn Grant Sale, is interviewed by World of Sport's Andrew Marriott.

1981 and it was the turn of the BBC to provide the cameras and technicians to cover two races for later transmission. In both years two giant car manufacturers had stepped in to add their names to the proceedings with Mazda Cars being involved at Rye House and FSO Cars taking the Donington meeting.

Television obviously offers huge exposure especially through its Saturday lunchtime sports spot and, thanks to the efforts of all concerned, Nick Brittan has over the last couple of years retained TV coverage of Superkart events at Donington screened by ITV. As the Superkarts have become more accepted, probably partly due to the TV coverage, so other programmes have occasionally given viewing time to the sport. The only lady competitor at World level in the 250 ranks, Carolynn Grant Sale, has appeared on breakfast TV and been involved in magazine type programmes.

The recent boom in home video recorders has provided another outlet for visual coverage of events and in this respect a number of companies and individuals have produced video cassettes for home use. Usually, all formats are catered for so you don't need to worry if your own video recorder is of one particular type; there will be a tape available to you. As stated earlier the impact that television can have with multi-million audiences opens up a vast area for those wanting maximum coverage at a reasonable cost. Within karting, advertisers and sponsors have probably not yet fully realised the advantages to be gained from such coverage but the signs are there that the message is getting through and it is hoped the future will see more and more of our sport on the box. Radio can also play its part in spreading the word and in that respect again it is left to local radio stations to include karting subjects in their programmes. Your own local station may well be prepared to include a spot on your own activities or a more general theme centred around the local club. Again if you want the local population to know of your successes then regional newspaper Sports Editors are often willing to give space to minority interests provided they are supplied with the necessary information. It's all worth a try so don't be afraid to give it a go; the more publicity the sport can get the better it will be for all involved. Remember that with most sports which

Video vision, motor sport video specialists seen filming Martin Hines at the 1982 Silverstone Kart Grand Prix.

Wherever your karting interest takes you, a magazine should be available. Language is no barrier as the pictures stay the same.

cater for a minority interest the media generally is reluctant to come to you. So if you are prepared to publicize yourself you will at the same time be getting the message across to the general public that the sport of karting does exist and that it is worth their taking an interest.

On a more international theme virtually all countries that participate in karting at any level do have their own specialist publications. These are not generally available on public sale in this country but can usually be obtained by subsription. You don't necessarily need to be multi-linqual to understand the contents; in any case the photographs are often worth looking at.

To summarise then, karting, although a minority interest especially as far as the national media outlets are concerned, does get quite well served by the specialist press. There is, of course, no reason why the information service should not improve and it is probably in the hands of the interested parties to really get out there and sell karting.

8 A Season's Competition

Jim and Kurt have been involved in karting for many years and Kurt already has, at the age of 21, nine years of racing experience under his belt. His father Jim successfully raced karts until the time came for him to concentrate more of his efforts on looking after Kurt's equipment.

The story behind Kurt Luby's successful 1984 defence of his British Long Circuit Championship for the 125 cc class really should begin two years earlier at the October Cadwell meeting. 1982 was quite a good year for the Lubys; Kurt ran well throughout the season finishing second overall in the British Championship. He did, however, score one notable victory and that came at the Grand Prix held on Silverstone's full circuit. After a terrific eight lap battle Kurt came out on top and took the coveted GP plates back home to Farnworth near Bolton in Lancashire. That was really the turning point for the father and son duo, for shortly afterwards they took the plunge and embarked on a programme aimed at designing and building their own kart chassis. They had previously used the ubiquitous Zip brand of chassis and their decision to go it alone was not due to any dissatisfaction with the outfit — indeed, they had enjoyed a fair amount of success — but just a strong desire to continue winning but to do that winning on a self-designed and self-built outfit.

The first step after that Silverstone victory had been to rough out their ideas on a piece of paper and it was soon after that when the first significant design change was introduced. Both Jim and Kurt accepted that there was little one could do to change the basic design of a racing kart chassis. Provision had to be made for engine mounting, rear axle and seat, etc. so most of their attention was aimed at the front end of the

chassis, and it was here that things began to change. Moving away from the conventional configuration Jim decided to go for an 'A' frame. The idea was not new, it had been tried many years earlier but before the advent of better and grippier tyres and good-quality tubing. The remarkable track hugging capabilities of a kart are not due just to its low centre of gravity and 'sticky' tyres; the flex built into the chassis also plays an important part. Jim felt that by going for the 'A' frame that all-important flexing would be centred

Father Jim: once a racer, now responsible for preparing the equipment used by Kurt.

Kurt was quite impressed with his first outing on a Phoenix at Cadwell in October 1982. A broken clutch, however, ended his day just after the start of the final.

a little further back resulting, it was hoped, in a stiffer front end. So out came the welding gear, and the ideas were transformed into an actual chassis or frame. The first two or three were not entirely to Jim's liking but eventually it all came right. A chassis was built up for that last Cadwell event to be held in October 1982. Prior to going to the Lincolnshire venue the outfit was tried on the short Three Sisters circuit near Wigan and the results were impressive. There were no fanfares, no brass bands, no shouting from the roof tops that this Luby creation was the best thing since sliced bread. They simply loaded up and went to Cadwell hoping that everything would turn out well.

Kurt was sufficiently impressed with the kart's handling during the meeting to believe that they were on the right lines. The winter of 1982/83 was to prove a busy time at the Luby premises as preparations were made for the 1983 season. A sponsorship deal had been struck with the Manchester-based Air Kilroe, an air freight company, and part of the package was the provision of a coach to be used as a mobile workshop and as transport to meetings. Production of chassis, now named Phoenix, was going on at a good rate in their somewhat cramped premises at Farnworth and enquiries were coming in from prospective customers. As the '83 season unfolded, Kurt was enjoying a good deal of success and at the end of the racing

The turning point. Kurt in happy mood after winning the Kart Grand Prix 125cc class in August 1982. Roy Patterson (left) and Boyd Barrington share the rostrum.

The Air Kilroe deal soon began to show when Kurt won at the 1983 Easter Cadwell.

Other competitors were soon showing an interest in the Phoenix chassis. This is one of the early customer examples in action at Snetterton.

year he had recorded seven outright wins. In addition to those victories he also had one third place, one twenty-first place and just three non-finishes. He won both the RAC Short and Long Circuit Championships for the 125cc class together with the Central Kart Club and Bridgestone 125cc Championships. The Phoenix was proving itself to be a winner and entry lists at meetings began to show more and more customers' examples on the grids.

The 1983 season wasn't without incidents though, and perhaps the worst experience was when the team coach destroyed its engine whilst on the way to Brands Hatch in July. That was also the weekend when Kurt was adjudged to have jumped the grid and his second place on the road suddenly became twenty-first. If that was the worst experience then perhaps the meeting Jim had with a Manchester-based businessman, Italian Salvatori Palmanterri, could be described as the point when the fortunes of the Lubys took a turn for the better. Salvatori, or Terri as he is affectionately known, asked Jim to build a kart just for fun, and in subsequent talks Jim was asked if he could build and sell karts on a commercial basis. The answer was a reserved

yes, Jim was already selling to customers albeit on a small scale and he felt that production could easily be increased providing he had larger and better premises together with some financial backing. Slowly but surely the idea began to take shape and before the end of 1983 a new company — The Phoenix Kart Manufacturing Company — had been formed, and negotiations were completed for a move to a new factory unit on the South Lancs. Industrial Estate near the Three Sisters kart track.

Taking into account all that the move entailed Kurt's performances on the track during 1983 showed that they could produce a high level of consistency. A second driver, in the shape of former Junior Champion Andy Cowgill, had been brought into the team at mid-season and, during the second half of the year, things were looking very promising for 1984. During the winter of 1983 another important development took place when Jim arranged to import an alternative 125cc engine. The motor in question was of Italian origin, the Minarelli, and hopes were high that it would be able to challenge seriously the all-conquering Austrian Rotax.

The first meeting of 1984 was as always

With Andy Cowgill netting a top three finish, the 1983 Short Circuit Championship at Fulbeck proved to be a happy and 'bubbly' occasion for the Team.

The refurbished coach provided a comfortable base at all meetings ... until it blew its engine on the way to Brands in July 1983.

Italian Businessman, Salvatori Palmanterri, affectionately known as 'Terri'.

scheduled for the Lincolnshire circuit Cadwell Park and the team arrived full of optimism for the new Minarelli engine. Talk around the paddock area was that the engine was not totally within the rules and it was thought likely that a protest would be made. That, however, was not to be, and the day's racing got under way with a lot of attention being directed at the Luby Phoenix camp. In the first heat Kurt had a slight misfire and, coupled with an excursion onto the Cadwell grass, he could only manage a sixth place. Kurt put his grass-cutting activities down to 'brain fade' and resolved to do better next time out. He certainly did that for after a good race with the Dino of Mark Allen he won the second heat in wet conditions. The final grid sheet appeared with the Number 1 plates of the Phoenix Minarelli outfit on the second row. Everything came good for the final and Kurt led the field home to record his first win of 1984. The problems, however, were only just beginning!

The question of the Minarelli's eligibility was referred to the RAC Kart Committee, and from there was passed on to the Technical Committee. The whole process took a considerable amount of time and for the next scheduled meeting on March 17th at Mallory Park the team had to revert to a Rotax engine. Having set themselves up in the expectation that the Minarelli would have no eligibility problems the team had hurriedly to acquire a Rotax engine and one was finally borrowed from a customer. After practice at the Leicestershire circuit all seemed well, the engine performed reasonably well but not quite up to the usual standards expected from a Luby-prepared motor. Pressure of work and the involved discussions regarding the Minarelli had meant that Jim and Kurt had not had sufficient time to prepare a suitable motor. Both heats that day resulted in the engine seizing and it was through the offer of another motor from Ian Shaw that Kurt managed to qualify for the final. He would, though, start from the back of the grid with a lot of work to do if he was to get a high finish. In all the rush to get on the grid the carb had been a little over-jetted and the final outcome was a third place in the final. Not a bad result considering all the problems the team had encountered over the weekend.

As the next event was also scheduled for Mallory and included a round of a Series for which Kurt had not been eligible to enter, a well earned break was taken, skiing in Austria.

Easter at Cadwell Park was the next meeting on the 1984 calendar and for that event the Luby Phoenix team was further increased when Kurt's mother Pat arrived at the circuit on the Sunday morning. Already present as always was Kurt's younger sister, Samantha and his young lady Wendy. Wendy assumes responsibility for the general well-being of the team at all events and works hard in keeping all personnel fed and watered. She purchases all the requirements for the coach kitchen prior to each meeting in addition to acting as team time-keeper during racing. The Easter weekend, however, was to turn out to be a disaster for the team and for Kurt in particular. Saturday night's practice and the Sunday morning had presented no problems but the first heat was when the worst happened. Having just taken the lead in the heat Kurt had a huge 'off' entering Park Straight, one of the fastest parts of the course. The kart careered off the track at great speed and finished up against the earth banking with Kurt still in the driving seat. The race was very quickly stopped and the emergency services were on the scene. Jim, from his vantage point a few hundred yards away, had realised something was wrong and could be seen sprinting up the banking on the inside of the circuit towards the stricken outfit. Kurt was removed from the kart and taken to nearby Louth hospital. He was found to have no bones broken but was suffering from shock and multiple bruises and it was decided to keep him in overnight for observation. Lying in that hospital bed Kurt reflected on the incident and recalled keeping his right foot hard down on the throttle in the hope that he could 'flick' the kart out of its problem. What he didn't realise at the time was that the cause of the accident had been a steering rose-joint failure resulting in the kart deciding its own path.

The scrutineers for the day decided after inspecting the damaged kart, that all Phoenix chassis entered would not be allowed to compete in the remainder of the meeting as they were all fitted with similar steering rose-joints to the one which had failed on Kurt's outfit. Jim, meanwhile, was unaware of that development as he was with Kurt at the hospital, but the decision to

The new factory premises close to the Three Sisters circuit near Wigan.

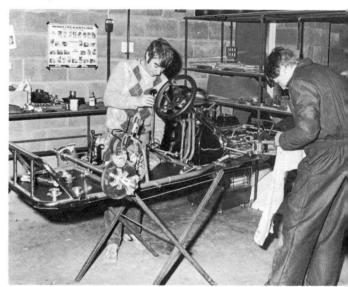
Once settled in their new premises late in 1983, it was down to some hard work.

Using the Minarelli engine, Kurt recorded his first win of 1984 at a very wet Cadwell Park.

It was back to the Rotax motor for Mallory in March, but with little time to fully prepare an engine, Kurt had to settle for third place.

Wendy also enjoyed some success in 1984 when she and Kurt became engaged later in the season.

After some detailed development work, this was the Phoenix full body creation.

stop Phoenix outfits racing was not a very popular move at the time. The officials' first consideration was for the safety of competitors and it was felt better to err on the side of caution than risk a similar accident.

The problem facing the team of how to get the coach and all personnel home to Farnworth in Lancshire, whilst leaving Kurt in hospital, was solved by an offer to transport Kurt home on the following morning providing of course he was given clearance by the hospital. The coach was duly driven across the Pennines and Kurt was left to spend the night in a hospital bed, arrangements having been made to collect him next day. On Easter Monday he was discharged from Louth hospital and, after enjoying a lunch of Lincolnshire sausages, he was driven home. The journey passed without incident and Kurt saw little of the scenery as he managed to rest his aching body and catch up on some sleep.

It was some time afterwards before Kurt was ready to admit just how much that accident had affected him, both in his mental approach to

Kurt in the lead at the Easter Cadwell, shortly before suffering a big 'off', resulting in an overnight stay in hospital.

racing and in the physical discomfort he suffered. Almost a full month passed before he was due to race again and it was back to Leicestershire and Mallory Park once again. Much work had been going on at the factory in developing a full body configuration for the Phoenix, and Mallory was to be its first real test. The meeting was also a round of the British Championship and Kurt was keen to pick up some points towards his defence of the Championship. At Mallory Park on May 13th Kurt finally had to admit that the Cadwell accident had knocked him quite severely. The team as a whole were under considerable pressure after Cadwell for they felt that they had something to prove. The new body appeared to work well but Kurt struggled all day, through the heats and in the final to finish eventually a disappointing 10th. He remarked afterwards, the kart was fine, the track was OK ... but the driver was well below form.

Whilst all this was going on Kurt was also being tempted into taking up an offer to enter the Formula Ford arena and tentative plans were being made to secure sponsorship which would give him a drive in the bigger Formula. The pressure was on. Only a couple of weeks after that Mallory meeting the kart fraternity moved to Donington Park for the prestige event, the World Cup. Although the main event is for the 250cc karts all the classes do derive some satisfaction from the meeting each year and winning is always nice. Being run to International Regulations the World Cup meeting allowed Jim and Kurt to bring out the Minarelli once more and see if they could repeat that initial success at the opening Cadwell meeting. Like Mallory the weekend turned out to be a bit of a disaster; too many changes were tried all at once and little appeared to be going right. The instructions from Italy regarding the battery output had been misinterpreted with the result that a smaller battery than necessary was being used. Despite all that a second row start was secured from the qualifying heats and there was just a chance that things might get better for the final. That was not the case, however, and Kurt had to be content with a lowly twelfth spot and more disappointment.

The next outing would have been at Cadwell Park in June but Kurt gave that one a miss as he followed up his car racing aspirations with a visit to Snetterton in Norfolk for the annual 24 Hour race. He had embarked on a training and fitness programme in order to get himself in top shape for the remainder of the season. Things were beginning to look a little better. The next outing for the Phoenix was a little closer to home for it was over the weekend of June 16th and 17th that Kurt visited Three Sisters for the Short Circuit Championships. Whilst the qualifying heats went reasonably well over the two days Kurt was

The first appearance of the full body at Mallory caused a few heads to turn but Kurt was not on top form after his accident.

At Donington for the World Cup, too many changes were tried at once and Kurt had a disappointing final.

Snetterton June 1984. A thrilling race for both drivers and spectators resulted in Kurt taking 9 more points on his way to the Long Circuit title.

At the Short Circuit Championship the heats looked good in Kurt's attempt to secure a hat trick of title wins.

After suffering fuel problems, Kurt finally retired from the Short Circuit final but found a comfortable spot from which to watch.

plagued by fuel feed problems and felt that all was not well. Sure enough Kurts defence of the Short Circuit Title did not last the distance and he was forced to pull off into retirement. That left him with just the Long Circuit Title and his efforts to retain that took him next to Snetterton in Norfolk for the third round of the Championship. Snetterton is a circuit visited by the karting world on only a couple of occasions each year, but it is a venue where Kurt usually does well. The weekend in June was no exception. Practice was arranged for the Saturday with the racing taking place on the Sunday and right from the start it looked good. The pressures of business were beginning to ease and for the trip to Norfolk Jim had gone back to the tried and trusted set up used previously. No new ideas were tried, this race was to be run for Championship points and it was felt the best way to approach it was in a proven way. On race day nothing really went wrong, Kurt secured pole position for the final and promptly won that as well to take a further nine points in the RAC Championship. The team returned to Lancashire in a much happier frame of mind.

Whilst Kurt had been the mainstay of the Phoenix Team two other drivers had been racing in the team colours during 1984. Andy Cowgill had been joined by ex-Superkart driver Jon Dixon, and for the next event they were joined by a visiting French driver, Jean Leret. Jon Dixon had enjoyed some success earlier in the year in winning an event at Mallory Park but his season began to fall to pieces and further good finishes were proving difficult to find. The Grand Prix weekend at Silverstone is always regarded as a 'one-off' meeting, often providing some unexpected winners. The Team was firmly established in a couple of the pit lane garages and all efforts were concentrated on getting a good result. Kurt had quite an eventful practice session, losing a wheel along Hangar Straight and narrowly missing the 100 yard marker board. Almost the same spot was to be the scene of Kurt being forced off by a backmarker in the first heat; the signs were not too good. By the time the qualifying heats were over Kurt found himself relegated to the last chance race in an effort to earn a place on the Final grid. In Jim's words, the weekend was one in which they were 'playing again.' Playing with different body configurations, different exhaust systems, all in an effort to overcome the unusual demands of Silverstone and its full 2.93 mile Grand Prix circuit. The final proved to be just a little too much and Kurt eventually managed to find his way into fourth place where he stayed to the flag. It was not a good weekend for the team but the prospect of almost a full month's break before the next meeting at least gave them time to try and sort out any problems. Before the next meeting came round it looked very much as if Jon Dixon would be taking no further part in the season and Andy Cowgill was about to hang up his racing leathers, too. Wedding bells called for Andy so by the time the next event at Cadwell Park loomed large on the calendar Kurt was running solo.

Cadwell Park was an important meeting for Kurt, he had to overcome any misgivings he might have after his Easter accident at the circuit. The first weekend in August was the time of the Cadwell event and it counted towards the RAC Championship. Kurt though, the defending Champion, only had nine points so in many ways the meeting was approached in an entirely different frame of mind. This one was for enjoyment only ... at least, that was the original intention. Practice on Saturday night gave Kurt the opportunity to push the Phoenix into Park Straight and finally get rid of any qualms he might have had regarding the accident. The evening passed without incident and it soon became obvious that Kurt was back on form. The heats on Sunday produced a second and a third place which earned him a second row start for the Final. Things were looking good and they were enjoying themselves. The Final proved to be a great race with half a dozen of the leading 125 drivers enjoying a terrific dice at the front. Kurt however

Ex-Superkart driver, Jon Dixon, didn't really stay with the Team long enough to prove his potential.

began to ease away from the rest and despite a strong challenge from Stephen Coward, another Lancashire driver, he took a deserved victory and added nine more points to his championship haul. The Final was at one stage producing as much entertainment off the track as it was on. Jim had positioned himself on the grass bank overlooking the main straight and as Kurt reeled off the laps and got the better of all the opposition Jim treated the crowd to some unrehearsed gymnastic activities as he ran up and down the bank in an effort to improve his view of the proceedings. Jim is always the first to admit that when he watches a race he only ever sees one driver ... and that is Kurt. The psychological battle with Cadwell had been won, Kurt was back on top form and two rounds of the Championship remained.

The first of those meetings took place at Mallory Park on September 9th and the weather that day couldn't have been worse. Practice and the heats passed off without too much of a problem though Jim decided to jet up for the Final. With about three hours to do that job, somehow things went a little wrong and, without realising at the time, the arm of the carb was refitted upside down. As the final got under way the weather got worse; the track was soon saturated and the very high winds blew across the circuit. The retirement rate was extremely high and Kurt's problems were not confined to the weather. That carb was inevitably playing up, and as the rain lashed down, Kurt was forced to attempt gear changing with his knee whilst fiddling with the fuel pipe in an attempt to get a reasonable flow. It was a difficult race and Kurt had to settle for ninth place and no further points towards the Championship. So it was a very wet Phoenix crew which made the journey back to Lancashire with the next Round of the Championship only two weeks away. That meeting was to be held at Snetterton, and Kurt has a liking for the Norfolk venue. The rain appeared to have followed the competitors to Norfolk for the race day was very very wet.

Phoenix on parade at Silverstone 1984 for the public Sunday morning walkabout.

All manner of things were tried at Silverstone, including the full body.

The practice day on Saturday was full of problems for Jim and Kurt as they struggled all day to get things right. The kart was well off the pace and Jim described Saturday as being A Hard Day's Night! The Rotax was not performing as it should and a couple of seizures necessitated stripping and rebuilding. The mood was not very optimistic for Sunday's racing but as things turned out the team's fortunes were about to change. The weather did little to help as it got progressively worse during Sunday and by the time the final came round it was pouring down. Kurt had enjoyed pretty good heats and lined up on the front row for the final. One of his main rivals, ex-Superkart driver Derek Price, commented before the off that if it did turn out to be wet then Kurt must be in with a good chance of nine more points and retention of the British Championship. What had been forgotten though was the fact that Ian Shaw could just pip Kurt for the title should Kurt not achieve a good result. It was almost a repeat of the 1983 Championship last round. As the lights flicked to green to start the final Kurt made an excellent start to get off the line first and lead the pack into the opening lap. As the laps were reeled off Kurt made great strides at the front increasing his lead with every lap. Acknowledged as a very good wet weather driver Kurt was demonstrating his capabilities in fine style. The rain got worse and worse but the Phoenix driver pressed on to run home a comfortable winner after ten very wet laps. Ian Shaw managed to grab second spot from Derek Price but as in 1983 had to settle for second place in the British Championship. The No. 1 plates were to stay in Lancashire on the Phoenix of Kurt and after an indifferent start to the Championship chase everything had turned out fine in the end.

The next meeting was just a week away and scheduled for Cadwell Park, but during that week Kurt and Wendy had more than the British Championship to celebrate. Wendy became 21 on the Thursday and her present from Kurt was a diamond engagement ring. So Cadwell was approached in good-humoured style, with the Cadwell Club having allowed Kurt to run the Minarelli engine on an experimental basis. The involved discussions on the Italian engine had been brought to a satisfactory solution with the news that it would be placed on the official list of approved engines as from November 1st, 1984. The event in Lincolnshire that weekend had been fixed for a Saturday rather than the usual Sunday, and the weather was to hold the upper hand at the start of the day. Fog shrouded the circuit and the organisers had to delay practice as visibility was almost nil in places. After waiting for a considerable time the decision was made to move the event to the shorter but, perhaps, more

Wedding bells called for Andy Cowgill during 1984 and he, like Jon Dixon, left the Team.

August brought a return to Cadwell Park and after a great dice with Stephen Coward, Kurt scored another fine win in the Championship class.

The 1984 RAC Championship was almost a repeat of 1983 with Kurt's main track rival again being close friend, Ian Shaw.

Snetterton, and the No. 1 plates are on the way back to Lancashire.

September Cadwell – a meeting which Kurt totally dominated using the Minarelli engine.

Shaws Hairpin at Mallory and Kurt proudly shows the No. 1 plates although he had to settle for third place on the day.

demanding, Woodlands circuit, and practice finally got underway. Almost immediately the Minarelli proved very quick and reliable with Kurt making a few heads turn as he negotiated the twists and turns of Cadwell Park. The heats passed without incident and once the fog lifted the day turned out to be dry and fine. In the first heat, Kurt started from the fifth row and after a good battle with Mark Webster he duly won. His performance in the second heat was even more impressive for from an eleventh row start he drove superbly to score a second win and claim pole position for the Final. The Final was almost a Luby

benefit for as the flag dropped to signal the start Kurt powered the Phoenix outfit off the line in tremendous style. By the time he reached the first corner, a tight right-hand hairpin, he had outdragged the rest to take a comfortable eight to ten lengths lead. By about half distance Kurt was encountering back markers and his lead looked to be in no danger whatsoever. He completely dominated the race and ran out a comfortable winner. As the Minarelli engine was being used, Kurt's victory went unrewarded for he was not eligible for any trophies. However, a great deal of satisfaction came with the victory and the knowledge that the Phoenix Minarelli combination was a winner.

Only one meeting remained in the 1984 season and that was to be held at Mallory Park on Sunday October 14th and once again Kurt was to use the Minarelli. The weather that day was excellent, sunny and dry, giving very good racing conditions with which to end the season. There was still much comment in the karting world regarding the Minarelli engine and Jim and Kurt were looking for one final victory to help silence the critics. The heats were not too successful, however, due to a wrong choice of gearing, but after Jim had played with his calculator, sorting out the ratios, things started to improve. A front row position for the final was achieved after the heat results and whatever the outcome the day was proving to be an enjoyable one under clear blue skies. At the off Kurt got a reasonable start and was quickly part of the scrap for second place. Just for a change Derek Price was the one to get a flier off the line and he very quickly secured a comfortable lead. Kurt meanwhile was battling furiously with two or three other drivers and throughout the race enjoyed a dice with arch-rival Stuart Ziemelis. Lap nine was the crucial point of the race for Kurt as a backmarker slightly slowed his progress and he had to be content with third place. Immediately after the meeting at Mallory Jim negotiated the sale of Kurt's outfit used on the day and thoughts turned to the winter ahead and preparation for 1985.

On reflection 1984 might not be thought an exceptional year, but when the facts and figures are looked at in more detail they still show that Kurt on the Phoenix is a winner. From fourteen meetings he took five outright wins, two third places and a fourth spot. The accident at Cadwell had quite an effect on the season with Kurt having to fight hard to overcome the results of that. Once he took that win at Snetterton in June though his fortunes took a turn for the better with three more victories from the next five meetings. His brief flirtation with Formula Ford also had a somewhat unsettling effect but once the decision had been made to stick with karting the results started to come again. Both Jim and Kurt feel that a 125cc kart does not get too much advantage from a full fibreglass body and their involvement with the development of the Phoenix version also caused a few unwanted problems. Customer enquiries regarding both Phoenix chassis and the Minarelli engine continued to come into the Phoenix works and Jim and Kurt received a substantial order from the United States of America to boost further their confidence in their own product. It was a big decision to go it alone in producing and racing their own brand of kart chassis but the results over the last two years have more than justified their faith in their own ideas. 1985 is viewed with a fair degree of optimism.

9 The World Series 1983

There have been one or two events in gearbox karting over the years which have proved to be classics as the years have gone by. In 1968 we had the first ever World Cup meeting on the short Heysham Head circuit and then in 1976 the inaugural European Championships for 250cc karts was held at Oulton Park in Cheshire. The organisation of both those events was in the capable and experienced hands of that Northern stalwart of gearbox karting, Bert Hesketh. As the 250s became quicker and more spectacular so interest grew in the prospect of holding a true World Championship on motor racing circuits.

Many European countries had taken to Superkarts and it was felt that the need was there to bring them all together in a multi-round championship to decide a World Champion. Serious moves to bring this about were made at the European Championships held at Donington in June of 1982. The President of the CIK, as we mentioned earlier, was a staunch supporter of the 250 scene and M. Buser called a meeting of all interested parties in an attempt to set the whole thing up. Initially it was felt that some European countries were not sufficiently experienced to stage such an event and the first suggestions were that all of the proposed rounds should take place in this country. That would of course have given British based drivers an advantage, certainly in knowledge of circuits likely to be used. It was also felt that European circuits would probably have to struggle to raise sufficient entries to make the idea work.

After long discussions in the corridors of power, however, both here and abroad, the decision was made to hold a World Championship in 1983. The Japanese tyre company, Bridgestone, stepped in to offer their valuable support to the series and with the full backing of the CIK the chase for the first official 250 World Champion was on. It was decided to add yet another special number plate to those already available to the 250 ranks; the winner of the series would be awarded the letter M. That coming from the French word for world: Mondiale.

For 1983, three rounds were arranged; the first to be held at the Jyllands Ringen circuit in Denmark in early June; the second one, a couple of weeks later, at Silverstone; and the final round to take place at the Paul Ricard circuit in Southern France in October. All three rounds would be held under CIK rules, described in an earlier chapter, and comprising timed practice, heats, a pre-final and then the final. In order that the event should live up to its 'world' title some entry qualifications were introduced in an attempt to bring only the very best drivers into contention. That didn't go down very well with some of our own regular long circuit competitors, for despite their apparent lack of success over the years many felt that their continued support of home events should have entitled them to take part. The series sponsors, Bridgestone Tyres, dug deep into their coffers and the series became a very lucrative one financially, at least to those who expected to do well.

So, with the cream of Superkart racing to be assembled in Denmark over the first weekend in June, the first round was looked forward to with eager anticipation. Twenty-two drivers from Britain were entered for the event and together with the attendant mechanics, wives, girl friends, officials and press, the journey from Harwich proved to be a convivial affair. One black cloud was left hanging over the docks though, as the main party began the trip across the North Sea. Space on the boat was at a premium and five drivers and their equipment were unable to get on the boat and were left on the quayside to await a later crossing. They did, however, make good use of the extra time ashore by drowning their sorrows in a local hostelry! Some of the drivers and their crews were booked in to hotels not far from the Jyllands Ringen circuit whilst others took their own accomodation in the shape of caravans or even tents. By Friday morning the paddock area of the circuit was buzzing as around 70 drivers representing nine countries prepared their outfits for the first timed practice session. Those left behind in England had been accomodated on a later sailing and duly arrived at the circuit late on Friday afternoon. They were late, unfortunately, too late to take part in timed practice and had to start their heats on the Saturday from the back of the grid.

For those who did take part in the timed session one man left no doubt in the minds of others that he was the driver to beat. The Hermetite Zip Team Leader, Martin Hines, proved to be the quickest at the end of the session and duly headed the time sheets. His time of 44.74 seconds for a lap of the 1475 metre circuit was only 3/100ths of a second quicker than Dutchman Perry Grondstra but nevertheless showed that with his prior knowledge of the anti-clockwise track he was a force to be reckoned with. The next best British names on the time sheets were those of the Dino UK driver, Steve Styrin, and the second Hermetite Zip team member, Reg Gange. Just ahead of those two in timed sessions was the Swedish driver, Lennart Bohlin. He, also, was no stranger to the Danish circuit and previous performances indicated that he would be well in the running.

As the weekend progressed and the heats were run, Martin Hines showed his earlier time was no fluke as he dominated the qualifying heats. In so doing he earned himself pole position for the first of the two finals which was to be over 15 laps of the track. Sharing the front row of the grid with the Hermetite Zip outfit was Steve Styrin, Dane Per Steffenen, Norwegian Torgje Kleppe and Swede Lars Johansson. Lennart Bohlin was on the second row after experiencing slight problems in the heats whilst Britain's Reg Gange would start from the third row. So at about two o'clock on the Sunday afternoon the scene was set and the pre-finalists assembled in the pit lane before being despatched on a rolling lap and then forming up on the grid to await the starter's signal. At the off it was Bohlin who got the best of it to lead the field into the first left-hander. He was closely followed by Kleppe, Styrin and another Dane, Poul Peterson. Martin Hines had

not got the best of starts and was running in about sixth place but about to make his move. At about half distance, 7 or 8 laps gone, Hines moved sweetly past leader Bohlin to take up the running. Kleppe, Styrin and Steffensen were still holding on to the next positions and the battle was hotting up. Three laps later and Hines, probably not realising it at the time, was out front on his own, Bohlin having retired leaving the Hermetite Zip driver with a clear advantage at the head of the field. Steffensen had also moved up a place to take second ahead of Kleppe with Styrin and Grondstra next. Other British drivers were performing admirably with Chris Lambden, Richard Dean and Reg Gange filling the next three places. Hines meanwhile motored serenely on towards the flag and another victory assured him of yet another pole position for the final to be held later in the afternoon.

The meeting also included some car racing on the programme and as the bigger machines took over the circuit to have their races so the kart drivers and mechanics busied themselves around the pit area. Frantic activity was seen in numerous camps as spanners were searched for to attempt

The founder of the World Cup at Heysham in 1968 – Bert Hesketh – was also behind the first ever European Championship in 1976.

Le Mans was a late replacement venue for the final round, which was due to be held at Paul Ricard in the South of France. Denmark and Britain hosted the other two rounds.

Dino UK driver, Ed Duckett (kneeling) did not automatically qualify for the Series, but a good result in a non-Championship event at Silverstone earned him the right to take part at Le Mans for the final round.

The entrance to Jyllands Ringen in Denmark; a popular venue and well known to many of the British contingent.

WALKIES! Security on race day was pretty tight in Denmark.

to put everything right for the final. This one would be of longer duration, 22 laps. Martin Hines was showing a fair degree of confidence as the time approached for the finalists to assemble once again. He knew that the man who might have been his biggest threat, Lennart Bohlin, was lanquishing well down the grid after that pre-final non-finish. But Lennart is recognised as a very experienced and capable driver, more than able to make up ground and be in a challenging position before many laps have been completed.

As the field rolled round to the start line thoughts of a British win, in the hands of Martin Hines, were uppermost in the minds of many observers. As the signal was given to start the race he didn't disappoint, the orange outfit screaming off the line to lead the pack away. Steve Styrin and Per Steffensen were in close attendance but by the end of one lap the order behind Hines was; Styrin, Petersen, Kleppe and Grondstra. More British drivers headed the next group, whilst Lambden, after a poor start was rapidly moving through the field. The race soon settled and by about half distance the racing was taking place in pairs, Hines leading, hotly pursued by Petersen; Styrin and Grondstra locked in battle for third place whilst Gange and Giles Butterfield were upholding British honour by filling the next two places. Bohlin had pulled out of the race with a failed clutch and Petersen was not really making much impression on Hines. Into the closing stages and Styrin was the next of the front runners

to suffer, like Bohlin he stopped out on the circuit with a broken clutch. Grondstra benefitted from that incident and he was then up to third place. Butterfield and Gange were still having a rare old tussle for fourth and fifth places, the advantage finally being held by Butterfield. Try as he did Petersen was unable to catch the flying Hines and at the flag the British driver was able to claim a maximum 15 points towards his quest for the World Title. Chris Lambden had overcome that terrible start to finish a very creditable ninth whilst the only lady amongst the entry, Carolynn Grant Sale took an excellent 12th place and was one of a number of drivers who suffered from aching muscles afterwards. The anti-clockwise direction of travel had put a strain on the body not previously encountered on British clockwise atracks. However, all the aches and pains of the weekend disappeared from the Hines camp happy with the result and with a new circuit record in the bag of a time of 44.45 seconds.

The celebrations carried on well into the night and as the British contingent reassembled at the quayside in Esbjerg for the homeward journey the mood was still a very happy one. By the time everyone arrived back in England there was a little over a week remaining before the second round was due at Silverstone. With points awarded down to twelfth place in each round the final result of the Danish event produced a table as follows;

Martin Hines – Britain	15
Poul Petersen – Denmark	12
Perry Grondstra – Netherlands	10
Giles Butterfield – Britain	9
Reg Gange – Britain	8
Torgje Kleppe – Norway	7

Other Britons in the points after that first round were Chris Lambden on 4 and Carolynn Grant Sale with just 1.

Since the start of the Grand Prix in 1978 the Silverstone weekend, with racing on the full 2.93 mile Grand Prix circuit, has become the highlight of the long circuit racing calendar. For 1983, not only was the Grand Prix catered for, but the meeting also included the second round of the World Series and the European Championship. The home-based drivers, not unexpectedly, went into this one with a high degree of confidence. In addition to the Superkarts, all national classes were included in the programme. Each having its own Grand prix and subsequent honour to the victor. The competitors began to arrive at the circuit as early as Wednesday prior to the event and the paddock area very quickly took on the appearance of a self-contained village. Transporters, vans, trailers, caravans, tents, all found a spot somewhere in the vast expanses of

Only 300ths of a second separated Britain's Martin Hines and Holland's Perry Grondstra after the timed session.

Dino UK driver, Steve Styrin, also ran well in the timed session.

The reason for Reggie Gange having to start from the third row of the pre-final; an unwanted sand pit stop.

Lennart Bohlin, Lars Johannsen and Stuart Ziemelis preparing for the main Final.

the Northamptonshire countryside. The pit lane garages were full to capacity with two, and sometimes three, drivers sharing one garage. Due to the previously-mentioned entry qualifications for drivers, a separate, non-championship event was included in the programme for those unable to gain entry to the main event. The CIK system of qualifying for the World Series round was again being used and timed practice was held on the Friday afternoon June 17th. The Series leader at this stage, Martin Hines, didn't have it quite all his own way in the session against the clock. Instead it was Sweden's Lennart Bohlin who posted fastest time breaking the 1 m 30 s barrier by just 1/100th of a second. Driving his Zip/Rotax with Loctite as the main sponsor the Swede looked very smooth and quick. Hines had to be content with second fastest time, almost a full second slower than Bohlin. Other British names to feature well in the time charts were; Nigel Smith, as extrovert as ever and with minimal assistance, displaying 'Space To Let' stickers on the bodywork of his Zip Rotax. A welcome addition to the scene and a driver who showed that he was more than capable of mixing it with the best at world level, was Brian Heery. Brian put up a couple of quick laps to take fourth fastest time. Reg Gange, Steve Styrin and Chris Lambden were also in the top dozen on the time sheets at the end of the session. Friday evening was, as usual at kart meetings, taken up by the search for that little extra tweak which might just bring an improvement to a driver's fortunes once the heats got under way on the Saturday. For some it was a case of major rebuilding work whilst others were able to fill the bill with just routine checks and maintenance. Of course, for those lucky enough to have free time on their hands a casual walk round the circuit offered a different view to that which they would see the following day. There was always the Silverstone clubhouse for those in need of liquid refreshment, although racing drivers do tend to save that sort of activity for the end of the meeting, either as a means of celebration or to drown their sorrows.

With the National classes sharing the meeting, the 250 Formula E drivers did, of course, have some breathing space between the heats once that section of the competition got under way on the Saturday. As the heats were completed the Swedish driver Bohlin was the man who earned pole position for the first of the two finals, which were to be held on the following day. Martin Hines had also performed well, as he did in the first round, and secured second spot on the front row alongside Bohlin. Next in line was the Dino UK driver Steve Styrin and alongside him appeared a controversial outfit, an all enveloping body around a Dino chassis, piloted by Norwegian Torgje Kleppe. This configuration had caused some ripples, in fact, even an appeal in Denmark, but after careful consideration by the officials had been approved, but only after a slight alteration to what were thought to resemble Formula 1-style skirts. Six laps of the full Grand Prix circuit would decide the result of the pre-final and determine the starting order for the nine lap final. That in turn would produce not just a new Grand Prix title holder but a new European Champion and give the winner 15 points towards the World Title.

There was a lot at stake then as the karts rolled up to the start line and as the green light appeared it was Brian Heery who got the best start with the rest in hot pursuit. At the end of one lap the Swede Bohlin had taken over at the front with Hines moving through to grab second spot. Heery, Dutchman Hartog, Lambden and Kleppe were next in line with Gange making rapid progress to find a place in the first ten. Hines gradually closed on the leader, Bohlin, and as they started the penultimate lap, number five, the orange Hermetite Zip took the lead. Gange had pushed through to third place and with the demise of Bohlin, who suffered tyre failure, that was soon to become second. Heery, Kleppe and Styrin were disputing that second spot with Gange and with Hines having pulled out a sizeable lead, interest was centred on that second place. At the completion of six hectic laps Norwegian Kleppe had edged in front of Heery to claim third behind Gange with Styrin in fifth place. Those five drivers would therefore make up the front row of the grid for the main final and the prospect of a good race was looking good. For those who had experienced problems time was at a premium as they and their spanner men worked like beavers in the pits to repair any damage.

So at about 4.30 on a fine Sunday afternoon the finalists were assembled in grid order in front of the main stands. An army of mechanics, pushers, well-wishers and photographers mingled with the drivers as the time approached for them to be sent off on a rolling lap of the 2.93 mile circuit. As they approached the lights at the end of that lap, the pace car pulled into the pit lane, the green light showed and the race was on. Within fifty yards disaster struck, for in the frantic search for that necessary grip and increase in speed half a dozen karts were involved in a multiple pile up and their drivers sidelined immediately. To further add to the confusion Hines, on pole position, had been delayed at the lights due to a marshall not leaving the track as quickly as he should have done. Amongst those involved in the multi-kart incident was one of the favourites for succes, the Swede Lennart Bohlin. The pack however had gone and picking up the lead for a quarter of a lap was Steve Styrin. Gange though was flying and as they appeared in view of the main stands to complete one lap he was in the lead. Heery was running strongly in third place with Kleppe hanging on grimly to fourth. Hines meanwhile was recovering well from that start line delay and with some excellent driving through the traffic hit the front on lap four. Kleppe and Styrin had also got the better of Gange, relegating the second orange outfit to fourth. As the race progressed so Hines hung on to his lead, but he was being chased and harried by the Norwegian Kleppe. Heery and Styrin were locked in battle for the next two places with Lambden, Goy and Kerkhoven disputing the next three places. Gange had suffered tyre failure and his race was over. More drama was to come, however, for as the leaders, Hines and Kleppe, started their penultimate lap Hines was visibly slowing and obviously in some sort of trouble. Into Copse, at the end of the main straight, and Hines' race was to finish in the catch fencing, like teammate Gange another tyre failure. That left Kleppe, in the fully-bodied Dino, out front on his own. Behind him came Styrin and Heery with a little gap before Lambden and Kerkhoven appeared. At the flag, after nine exciting laps, full of incident, Kleppe took the honours with British entries completing the top five. A somewhat surprising victory for the Norwegian and disappointment for first round winner Hines, but as they say, 'to finish first, first you have to finish.' When all the points were totted up the positions after the second of three rounds looked like this;

Torgie Kleppe — Norway	22
Martin Hines — Britain	15
Steve Styrin — Britain	12
Poul Peterson — Denmark	12
Chris Lambden — Britain	12
Perry Grondstra — Netherlands	10
Brian Heery — Britain	10

Only two drivers, Kleppe and Lambden, had scored points in both rounds, and with a bonus prize at the end of the series for anyone scoring in all three they were looking forward to the final deciding round in France in October with some confidence. The Series so far had lived up to its promise and one or two drivers expected to do well had suffered problems whilst some not thought to be in the running at the start of the Championship had after Silverstone caused a few shock waves.

There was quite a lengthy time gap before the final round was due, it was in fact scheduled for the weekend of October 15th and 16th at the Paul Ricard circuit in the South of France. The domestic competitions, meanwhile, provided the drivers with their usual quota of race meetings whilst in the background rumours and counter rumours came to the surface regarding the venue for that final deciding event. After much discussion the decision was eventually announced that Paul Ricard would not host the event and it was to be moved to world famous Le Mans and held on the Bugatti circuit.

A smaller than usual entry assembled in

Martin Hines soon took the lead in the final and is seen here heading Styrin (35), Per Steffenson (5), and Poul Petersen (1) out of the first corner.

Perry Grondstra showed good form all weekend in Denmark to take third.

After a terrible start Chris Lambden recovered well to claim ninth.

France for the October weekend with Britain again having the largest number of representatives; a total of 21. Eight other countries were present but a number of drivers who had not scored in the previous two rounds decided to give it a miss. The usual procedure of timed sessions, heats and two 'finals' was on the cards and as the time sheets were posted up at the end of those initial runs a familiar name appeared at the top. As he did in Denmark Martin Hines had recorded the quickest time, 1m 39.18s, with two more Britons, Brian

Heery and Roger Goff, making up the top three. Lennart Bohlin was next on the time sheets followed by Dutchman Stolk. Gange and Sandy Dalgarno were next up with Series leader Kleppe, Styrin and Lambden completing the top ten.

As the heats got under way on the Saturday many of the top names experienced problems. Hines, Styrin, Kleppe and Heery all had either engine or gearbox problems resulting in non-finishes, and necessitating time consuming rebuilds or even replacements. With a repeat

The spoils of victory for Martin Hines with Poul Petersen and Perry Grondstra looking on. The young lady seems more interested in the onlookers.

The Silverstone pit and paddock area was full to capacity for the second World Series round in June.

After posting fastest time in the early qualifying session, Swede Lennart Bohlin needed a helping hand from fellow countryman Lars Johannsen when he struck problems in a heat.

Steve Styrin aboard the more conventional Dino secured a front row start for the final.

Brian Heery showed excellent form at Silverstone and is seen here leading eventual winner Torgje Kleppe.

Brian Heery leads the pack into Copse Corner at the start of the pre-final.

Blast off for the main final at Silverstone with Brian Heery just getting the jump.

Tyre failure forced Lennart Bohlin out of the pre-final.

performance of his Silverstone form Swede Lennart Bohlin was the name to emerge with pole position for the first of the finals. Two heat wins had assured him of that. One or two surprises appeared in the top ten and with the previously mentioned 'star' names lanquishing towards the back of the grid it was the turn of Dutchman Stolk, Scot Sandy Dalgarno, another Dutchman, Perry Grondstra, and Englishmen Goff, Derek Price, Butterfield and Glenn George to claim a place on the first two or three rows for the final. Hines was down in twenty-second place; Gange, twenty-eighth; Heery thirty-seventh and points leader Kleppe in forty-fifth spot. If Kleppe was to maintain his lead and take the title he was going to have a lot to do; but then so was Hines if he was to challenge the Norwegian for top honours. Bohlin was the man with the advantage at this stage as he had that pole position but as the grid

The multiple shunt only seconds after the start of the main final with Bohlin at this stage clear of the action.

Bohlin (No. 47) about to be T-boned by Allan Krownow with No. 49 offering a helping hand.

The aftermath. Drew Liddle (far left), Lennart Bohlin (centre), and Allan Krownow (right) survey the damage. Their race is over —fortunately without personal injury.

Lap four and Hermetite Zip Team Leader, Martin Hines, had put in an excellent drive to hit the front.

was assembled at about 2.30 on the Sunday afternoon the question was: who could challenge the Swede for supremacey and earn a good grid position for the main final yet to come? As the lights changed to green it was front row man Stolk who got the best of it ahead of Goff and the rest. Bohlin was already in trouble and dropping down the field at an alarming rate. Hines meanwhile had got a storming start and by the end of that first lap was up to third place ahead of Grondstra. As the laps passed so the battle raged; Goff, Stolk and Grondstra were the leading trio and positions were being swapped constantly. Hines was lurking in fourth place ready to take advantage of any slips by that leading threesome. Bohlin was in serious trouble and coasting round near the back of the field. Kleppe was to go missing as was Heery and it was becoming a race of numerous retirements. Dalgarno, Petersen, Styrin, Carolynn and Derek Price were filling the places immediately behind the leaders and as the race reached its closing stages Grondstra made his move and slipped by Goff to take the lead; an advantage he held to the flag. Goff, therefore, had to be content with second whilst Hines had driven an excellent race to claim third ahead of Stolk. With the finishing order determining the starting order for the main event, that result put Hines in a strong position. Especially in view of the fact that his closest rival for the title, Kleppe, had not finished, nor had Bohlin or Heery. Those three would start the final from lowly grid positions with a tremendous amount of hard driving to do to get in the points. With only about an hour between the end of the pre-final and the start of the final those who had experienced problems had a lot to do in a minimum of time to ensure they were able to take their places on the grid.

At about a quarter to four the finalists duly lined up in their respective positions and were led out on a rolling lap by the course car. As the signal was given for the 'off', Hines it was who got a flier. Incredibly both Bohlin and Heery also got a tremendous start from their poor grid positions and were both quickly right up with Hines and following his every move. As the race progressed the spectators were treated to an excellent battle of wits at the front between those three. Behind the leaders the fight for the places was being staged in pairs with Goff and Stolk disputing fourth place; Dalgarno and Petersen sixth and seventh whilst Carolynn was succeeding in holding off Styrin. Lap six and the picture at the head of the field began to look a little different. Both Bohlin and Heery had at last found a way past Hines and in a flash he was relegated to third spot. Kleppe meanwhile was running in about tenth spot and looked to be posing no real threat to the leaders as the race reached its closing

Fifth, sixth and seventh places were being hotly disputed by Chris Lambden, Mick Goy and Rob Kerkhoven.

A new style combine harvester? Martin Hines suffered tyre failure on the penultimate lap when leading the main final and this was the result.

Derek Price and the Stratos overcame problems at Le Mans and started from a good grid position in the pre-final.

After Hines' retirement, Kleppe took first spot and held it to the flag. Victory gave him the European title, British Grand Prix title and 15 points in the World Series.

The first three, Kleppe, Styrin and Heery, about to sample the spoils of victory.

Giles Butterfield was one of a number of drivers with some work to do before the final.

Brian Heery recorded quickest time at Le Mans, underlining his strong showing at Silverstone.

Roger Goff (14) made a good pre-final start and quickly got ahead of early leader Stolk (64).

Perry Grondstra of Holland overhauled Goff in the closing stages to win the pre-final.

With the rolling lap completed, the field edges towards the line waiting for the green light.

stages. As the last lap was started Bohlin still had the advantage, Heery was just ahead of Hines but the latter pair were constantly changing places. Out of the last corner to the finishing line and Bohlin still hung on, and as they flashed down the short straight to the flag Heery managed to find that little extra to snatch second from Hines. Stolk still had the better of Goff at the end with Carolynn, tyrin, Grondstra and Price next in the finishing order. Kleppe who had started the weekend seven points clear of Hines was next, in 10th place, and that was enough to earn him three points and allow Hines to draw level and equal his points total of 25.

The first ever official CIK World Championship had ended in a tie. Out came the rule books

Martin Hines got a flyer off the line but was quickly being shadowed by No. 70 Lennart Bohlin.

Scot Sandy Dalgarno (8) and Dane Poul Petersen (34) disputed sixth and seventh places in the main final.

Lennart Bohlin got the better of Hines by lap six with Heery closing fast and about to do likewise.

Carolynn Grant Sale showed excellent form to take sixth spot in the main final.

Martin Hines shares his moment of glory with father Mark.

Disappointment for Kleppe. Despite finishing in the points he could only match Hines' total, the Championship going to the Hermetite driver by virtue of his higher finishing positions.

Hines (centre); Bohlin (left) and Heery in happy mood after receiving their trophies at Le Mans.

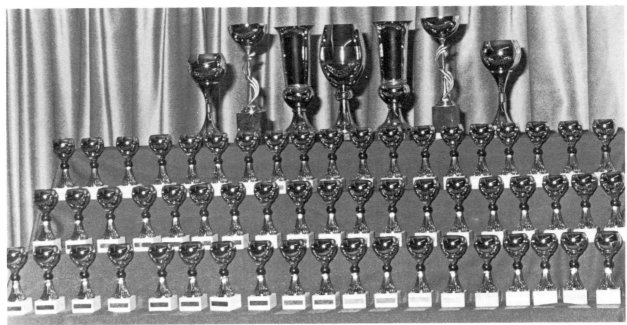

The impressive array of trophies at Le Mans with all competitors receiving a souvenir to mark their participation in the event.

and after some deliberation the verdict went to Martin Hines, the decision being based on the next best score after each driver's win had been taken into account. Hines had that win in Denmark and a third place at the last round. Kleppe had recorded a victory at Silverstone and a seventh place in Denmark so the World Title was on its way back to Britain. M for Mondiale would adorn the Hines outfit for the following year; or should it be M for Martin! After all the celebrations had died down and the crews made their way home the final points table for the inaugural World Championship looked like this;

Martin Hines — Britain	25
Torgje Kleppe —Norway	25
Brian Heery — Britain	22
Steve Styrin — Britain	18
Perry Grondstra — Netherlands	15
Lennart Bohlin — Sweden	15
Poul Petersen — Denmark	14
Chris Lambden — Britain	12

Due to the increasing use of electronic timing equipment at major events, and the greater difficulty in displaying characters than numerals, it was later decided that the new World Champion Martin Hines would not carry the letter M denoting his title but would instead display a red No. 1. That follows the established pattern in 'special' No. plates as both the European Champion and World Cup title holders have red.

10 The Drivers

With around 200 entrants at most long circuit meetings each year we could not possibly hope to include everyone in the following pages. What we have tried to do is bring you those names which feature most regularly in the results sheets. In doing this we hope those drivers not included don't feel that we are writing them off as no-hopers. Indeed, without the supporting cast there would be no winners. Being gentlemen through and through we have started the section with the only lady to compete regularly at world level in the 250 ranks, Carolynn Grant Sale, and her Hermetite Zip outfit. We then play it safe and list the remainder in alphabetical order, you can draw up your own list in order of merit.

Carolynn Grant Sale

Carolynn is the only lady driver regularly competing at the top level of Superkarting. A member of the Hermetite Zip Team, she prefers to be assessed as just a driver rather than a 'lady driver'. Results have confirmed that she is a very capable pilote frequently finishing in the top ten against the best in the world. She was second overall in the 1981 British Championships and ran well in the CIK World Series of 1983. She recently tried her hand at car racing at the wheel of a Clubmans Sports machine.

Mark Allen

Mark can always be relied upon to give his best and usually scores some high finishes in both the 125 class and the 210s. A former short circuit British Champion and a very capable and experienced driver.

Phil Ansell

Based in Blackpool his Ansell Prepared Villiers (APV) have assisted a number of drivers to many successes in that class. Phil won the 210 class Grand Prix in 1980, is a former British Champion in the Villiers class and is now running a Zip GP in the Superkart category with some regular top ten finishes. A nasty shunt at Silverstone in 1983 brought his racing season to a premature end but he was back in the driving seat for 1984.

Boyd Barrington

Twenty-three years old and based in Suffolk, Boyd lists his only interest as karting and the more the better! Second at Silverstone in the 125 class in 1982 Boyd had a difficult year in '83. Campaigns an Ian Rushforth Spyda chassis having previously been seen aboard a Lancer. As with so many others in this day and age, finance is always a problem but when things are running well he is usually not far away from the front.

Malcolm Belbin

A twenty-four year old Aero Development and Test Engineer from St. Albans, Malcolm is one of the newer members of the Superkart ranks. He started racing on his 16th birthday and moved from 210 National to Superkarts in 1982. He performed well in his first year at that level but his appearances in 1984 were limited through lack of funds. Now campaigns an EDR outfit from the Ed Duckett stable.

George Bett

A very experienced 210 competitor, George is a radio and television retailer in Thornton, Fife. He does most of his own preparation and has been rewarded with the Scottish Championships on eight occasions. He totally dominated the Villiers class in 1984, winning both the Long and Short Circuit Championships and the Grand Prix.

Lennart Bohlin

The Super Swede, Lennart has a long list of wins to his credit and is regarded as one of the best within the sport. Four times winner of the World Cup at Heysham, seven times Swedish Champion and European Champion in 1980, his record speaks for itself. He went one better in 1984 and won the CIK World Title being the only driver to score in all four rounds. An excellent ambassador for karting wherever he appears, he carried the colours of BP Sweden during '84 having previously enjoyed the sponsorship of Loctite.

Richard Boston

Richard settled into just one class, the 250 National, last year after previously campaigning in the 210 class as well. He was always at the front and one of the drivers to give the dominant Peak Revs team something to worry about as he ran well aboard the Dino. A former 210 Grand Prix winner, Richard is now concentrating on the 250 scene with Robbie Kellett ably supporting him as spanner man.

Giles Butterfield

A twenty-one year old engineering student with an eye on Formula Ford 2000, Giles started racing a 210 class kart on short circuits in 1980. He continued in the class on long circuits in 1981 moving up to the Superkart ranks late in 1982. He carries the colours of his father's restaurant — The Rugby Club of London — on his Zip GP, but 1983 was a disastrous year as far as results go with very few finishes recorded.

Giles enjoyed a much better season in 1984 scoring points in three rounds of the World Series to finish in joint fourth place overall.

Alan Cheetham
The man behind the Peak Revs business and winner of the 250 National Class Grand Prix in 1983. Along with Derek Rodgers and backed by Leaside Tyres, Alan dominated the single cylinder class in 1983. Has not been seen in racing leathers quite so often in 1984, as he concentrated on the engine preparation side of things for the Leaside Team.

Stephen Coward
At twenty-five years old Stephen has been racing for around eight years during which time he has won the 125 class Short Circuit Championship. A surprise winner of the 1981 Grand Prix for the 125 category he then got himself married and went into 'temporary' retirement, only to come back with a bang in the 1983 Grand Prix when he finished second. Stephen has ambitions to own his own kart business.

Sandy Dalgarno

The other half of the Rob Kerkhoven Racing team, Sandy lives near Aberdeen and consequently puts in a lot of miles just travelling to meetings. A very determined driver who has an enthusiastic approach to his karting activities, he finished fourth in the 1981 European Championships held in Sweden.

Richard Dean

Richard has been racing karts since 1974 and is a self-employed baker and confectioner from Ripley in Derbyshire. He moved to Superkarts from 210 National and has usually been a top ten runner. The high spot of 1983 was his win in the prestigious World Cup and the right to display the Zero plate. As things turned out Richard became the last driver to win that event at Heysham as 1984 brought a change of venue to Donington.

Mike Doble

Mike is an experienced competitor having recently moved into the 250 National class from 125s. He immediately stamped his mark on the class consistently appearing in the top six and taking three wins. He was winner of the 250 National Grand Prix at Silverstone in 1984.

Tim Doble

The name Doble has been around the kart tracks for many years and Tim carries on the tradition in the 210 class. He started racing at the age of 13 in non-gearbox karting. 1982 was his first year on the long circuits and, starting the season on novice plates, he ended it as the British Champion in his class. Based in Surrey, Tim is married with one daughter and lists his only hobby as being ... karting!

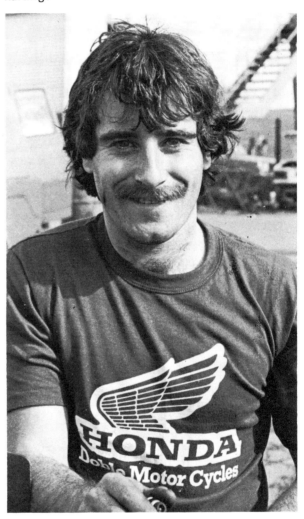

Reg Gange Jnr

One of the best-liked characters at the top level of gearbox karting, Reg has over 20 years experience in the sport. He is always willing to give sound advice to newcomers. Once a member of the National Junior Team, Reg was British and Southern Champion in 1971. He moved to the 250 class in 1973 and won the World Cup that year, repeating that success in 1981 and going on to win the Grand Prix in 1982 in devastating style. Regarded as being an excellent wet weather driver and one of the last of the late late brakers his fellow competitors have a great deal of respect for him. He won the European Championship in 1984 and finished second overall in the CIK Bridgestone World Series. For the last couple of years Reg has been racing with the Hermetite Zip Team and on his day is a very difficult man to beat. A partner in a garage business in Surrey, a game of pool provides Reg with some alternative relaxation. ►

Roger Goff

Roger has served a long apprenticeship in non-gearbox and short circuit 125 racing. He moved up to Superkarts and long circuits a couple of years ago and almost at once was very competitive. Has regularly featured in the top six during 1984 and has undoubted ability.

He finished equal 4th in the CIK Bridgestone World Series in 1984 and won both the 125 and 250 Formula E short circuit titles in June at Three Sisters near Wigan.

Perry Grondstra

Hollands' Mr Karting, Perry is a former Dutch Champion, who, though only 20 years old, has had ten years experience. He showed well in the 1983 inaugural CIK World Series finishing fifth overall.

1984 was a very mixed year for Perry, his best result being a sixth spot in the World Series round at Le Mans in September.

Brian Heery

A motor trader from Cheshire, Brian first took to the little wheels in 210 Villiers and had many successes culminating in his winning the Grand Prix for 210s in 1979.

He moved up to Superkarts in 1980 and is usually amongst the front runners. Business commitments curtailed his racing activities at the start of the 1983 season but towards the end of the year he put in some excellent drives; second at Silverstone; winner of the TV Times Challenge round in July and second in the last round of the World Series. 1984 began with a fine win out in South Africa ... again in the World Series and he followed that up by winning the World Cup and coveted Zero plates at Donington in May 1984.

Martin Hines

Without doubt the best known name in karting circles in this country. From Juniors to 1983 World Formula E Champion this man has seen and done it all ... well almost. With his father he has built up the successful Zip Kart business supplying karts and accessories world-wide. A keen eye for publicity and always the innovator he has been at the forefront of long circuit karting since its early days. Over the years Martin has won just about every title available with the exception of the World Cup. He is a former European Champion and became the first officially recognised CIK World Champion in 1983, was British Champion in the class for the last two years and Grand Prix winner in 1984. Karting is Martin's life and he has done a tremendous amount of work in furthering the cause.

Rob Kerkhoven

A Garage Proprietor from Worcester, Rob is another very experienced driver. He started racing way back in 1965 and has been a regular front runner for many years being European Champion in 1981 and British Champion on no less than five occasions. Along with Scot Sandy Dalgarno Rob forms the RKR Team and campaigns a Zip/Rotax.

Torgje Kleppe
An infrequent visitor to these shores, this
Norwegian driving instructor surprised almost
everyone with his victory at Silverstone in 1983
which landed him the European and Grand Prix
Titles. In addition he took maximum points in the
World Series round making the finale in France
later in the year a real cliff hanger. He earned
praise from many of his fellow competitors for the
way he handled the 'nervous' looking full bodied
Dino. His 1984 season was almost a disaster
when compared to 1983. He relinquised both the
European and Grand prix titles and scored only
three points in the World Series.

Bill Longden

Bill has campaigned a 210 self-tuned outfit for a number of years with many successes. His Longtune variety of engine is used by a good many drivers in the 210 class.

A former British Champion, Bill has spent some time away from the circuits during the last two years. However his two wins at Donington and Cadwell in 1984 proved that he is still a very capable driver.

Kurt Luby

Kurt has packed a lot of experience into his nine years of kart racing. He won both Long and Short Circuit 125 Championships in 1983 and retained the long circuit one in 1984. With his father, Jim, he runs the Phoenix Kart Manufacturing Company within a stone's throw of the short circuit at Three Sisters near Wigan. Highly regarded by all of his fellow competitors he is equally at home in wet or dry conditions. A real racer's racer.

Andy Martin
From the North East of England, the Car and Karting Centre driver covers a fair mileage in attending meetings. Has quickly established himself as one of the front runners in the 210 Villiers class and scored three victories in 1984.

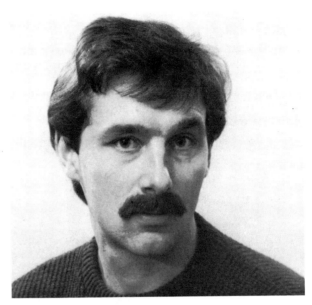

John Newton
Director of a Garage business in Petts Wood, Kent, John started racing in 1974 and has been British 210 Champion on three occasions: 1979, 1981 and 1983. He also won the 210 Grand Prix in 1983. His preparation is always meticulous, checking and re-checking until he is sure everything is to his satisfaction. That attention to detail has paid dividends; he dominated the 210 class in 1983 and, having moved on to 250 National for 1984, consistently scored top ten finishes.

Alan Ogden

Twenty-five year old Londoner Alan had a spell in Formula Ford with limited success. Since joining the 210 ranks in karting has usually figured in the top seven or eight. He was National Judo Champion at the age of 15 and enjoys a game of squash in addition to taking an interest in other forms of motor sport.

Poul Petersen

Well known for his unique self-built PVP chassis, Poul is a precision engineer in his home country of Denmark. Four times Danish Champion and European Champion in 1979, he has not always enjoyed the best of fortunes when competing on British circuits.

Derek Price

Derek had a successful time in non-gearbox karting at national and international level before moving to the gearbox class. Had a spell in Superkarts with some success but due to lack of funds moved back to the 125 category for 1984. With the help of John Stephens and Euro Kart Racing, Derek quickly showed that he is more than capable of mixing it with the best. His win at Mallory Park towards the end of 1984 confirmed that.

Derek Rodgers

Having a keen sense of humour, Derek can be relied upon to see the funny side of karting. Nevertheless, when behind the wheel of his 250 National outfit he is a very difficult man to beat. To Derek coming second is almost as bad as not finishing at all, such is his determination. He campaigned Superkarts until a couple of years ago when financial restraints forced him to give up the big class. British Champion in the 250 National class in 1983 and 1984, Derek looks like moving back up to Superkarts in 1985 with his present backers, Leaside Tyres.

Ian Shaw

Ian saw his first ever kart in a shop window in Chesterfield and was hooked from then on pestering his parents to buy one. He started racing in the Junior classes at the age of fifteen moving to 125s on short circuits and thence onto the full motor racing circuits. The only driver to score in all six rounds of the 1983 British Championships, even then he had to settle for second place overall. Ably assisted by Derek Price in the preparation department during 1983 his consistency paid off when he was offered a Zip supported drive for 1984.

Chris Stoney

Another vastly experienced driver in both short and long circuit competition, Chris was double British Champion in the 250 National Class in 1982 then turned his attentions to the 125 class. His wife also competes on short circuits in the 125s. Chris says he does not like racing for money, preferring the enjoyment and satisfaction in winning. His record has brought him plenty of that.

Steve Styrin

A highly-experienced driver, Steve is a former British Champion and Grand Prix title holder. A very quiet person off the track, Steve was once referred to as the man who grew horns when in his racing leathers! He is without doubt very determined and very competent, showing excellent form during 1984 aboard the Ed Duckett EDR when he secured a number of wins.

Stuart Ziemelis

Last but by no means least, Stuart has been at the front of 125 racing for the last few years. Former British Champion on both long and short circuits, he has his own tuning and preparation business, with Super Swede Lennart Bohlin listed as one of his customers.

Dubbed Super Stu after his dominance of the 125 scene, the 1984 season was one of mixed fortunes for this quiet-mannered driver. Stuart, however, has had a consistently good record over many years and a successful 1985 season would come as no surprise.

Useful Addresses

The RAC Motor Sports Association Ltd,
31, Belgrave Square,
London,
SW1X 8QH

Commission Internationale De Karting,
8, Place de la Concorde,
75008 Paris,
France.

Kart and Superkart Magazine Ltd,
Pindar Road,
Hoddesdon,
Hertfordshire.

Karting Magazine,
Bank House,
Summerhill,
Chislehurst,
Kent.

Motoring News,
Standard House,
Bonhill Street,
London,
EC2A 4DA.